# THE ULTIMATE
## ECOMMERCE
## EMAIL & SMS
# PLAYBOOK

The Complete Guide to Unlocking Profitable,
Predictable and Sustainable Revenue Streams
from Every One of Your Customers.

ISAAC HYMAN

ISBN: 9798836245603

# BONUS MATERIALS

### Free Online Workbook, Guides & Starter Kit

This book is packed with market data, strategies, and tactics for creating a highly profitable, predictable and sustainable revenue stream using email, SMS and CRM. I've implemented every step of these strategies successfully to grow email & SMS revenue by 300% or more for 7, 8, 9 and billion dollar brands. I'm on a mission to help level the playing field for small yet scaling e-commerce brands so I've packaged up all our email, SMS and CRM playbooks, workflows, guides and webinars into one HiFlyer LaunchPad Kit, exclusively for buyers of this book and valued at $4,995. You can download our entire Launchpad kit for free by visiting HiFlyerDigital.com/launchpad. I highly recommend you keep the LaunchPad Kit handy and complete the documents as you go through this book.

# RAVE REVIEWS

In our most recent year, Isaac achieved 50% revenue growth while reducing volume by 40%. He's remarkably well-suited to manage any e-commerce email, SMS & CRM program.

**Lev Peker, CMO**
**Adorama**

Isaac's email, SMS and CRM expertise was instrumental in our three-year customer-centric strategy and he excelled in communicating, implementing and achieving the vision we set forth.

**Barry Litwin, CEO**
**Global Industrial**

It's been one of the best decisions I've made in the last couple of years hiring you all! Your expertise is awesome. I know we're still getting started but HOT DAMN we have an awesome road ahead of us.

**Debbe Simmons**
**BicycleWarehouse.com**

What impressed me most about you was that you had a plan. And it was bigger than I thought it would be. I'm so glad I hired you. You promised we would get to 30% of revenue and that's exactly what you did. I see now that I should've started a long time ago.

**Cindy Harris, Owner**
TheJewelryVine.com

My line was email marketing was dead… but if there was someone who could do it well, it was you. We've gone up in revenue well over 100% since we started working together. It's our fastest growing revenue stream. We were at 1% of revenue; now it's well over 25%. If you had hesitations like I did or you were uncertain if you'd see an ROI or if you've been burned before… trust Isaac.

**Yitzi Gruen, Owner**
JudaicaPlace.com

Working with Isaac and his team helped fill the void that our publisher wasn't able or willing to fill. We would never have sold 25,000 copies as fast as we did without the help of him and his agency.

**Benis & Robert Reffkin**
*No One Succeeds Alone* book

# TABLE OF CONTENTS

This book is dedicated to my beautiful wife, Olivia, and my four gorgeous children Suri, Ben, Aliza and Nathan.

Without your love and encouragement, I never would've learned how life-changing a great relationship can be

# PREFACE

I decided to go all-in on agency life during the most challenging work environment of our lives: the COVID-19 pandemic.

Like millions of other businesses, the e-commerce retailer I worked for was hit hard during the pandemic. Let's face it: no one is buying high-end cameras, lenses, and electronics when struggling to keep their job in a hard-stop economy and adapting to work-from-home life.

At the time, I compared the world to a snowglobe. Everything in our tiny world was shaken, stirred, and in a state of flux. Everyone was pivoting; schools were closed, jobs were lost, and whole states were shutting down. No one knew what the future held, and no one could forecast when life would get back to normal.

I had friends and family members who were left without jobs, stability, or savings. For those who remember that 90-to-180-day period after the COVID-19 shutdowns were announced, you probably felt that there was a universal state of panic.

Until COVID-19, I preferred running side hustles where clients would pay me a few thousand dollars here and there for some e-commerce strategies and execution. No major headaches, no weekly check-in calls, and no team hires. Combined with a full-time, six-figure job, I was pulling in a great income and maintained a comfortable lifestyle. It was all so simple before COVID-19.

But while COVID-19 was occurring, I did know one thing: like a shaken-up snowglobe world, those little snowflakes were still up in the air, slowly falling into place. For those who are natural entrepreneurs or visionaries like myself, you view a state of uncertainty as one thing: an opportunity.

Naturally, I was determined to see COVID-19 as the catalyst for a new opportunity and pivot into a new life, one where I was in control of my finances, freedom, and focus.

With the encouragement of my wife and family, I embarked on the arduous yet exciting path of marketing agency ownership. I had my work cut out for me. I'm blessed with a wife and four children, so, for their sake, I didn't have time to wing it or do a 14-day trial on this. I needed to be all in and start scaling fast.

To the outsider looking in, this was one of the worst times to be a marketing agency owner. Marketing budgets were being cut, whole departments were being cut, and stalwart businesses were shutting down. And although I'm a natural salesperson and seasoned marketer, I knew very little about - nor did I excel in - agency operations, fulfillment, and scaling beyond a few dozen clients.

And my inexperience showed. After grabbing a handful of clients in 90 days, I quickly scaled to $25,000 in monthly recurring revenue (MRR), only to see a third of them leave after ninety days because I was stretched too thin. I couldn't keep up on fulfillment for clients in different industries with different marketing needs.

So, towards the end of 2020, I took a step back and refocused on my core competencies: helping e-commerce brands build better customer relationships using email, SMS and CRM. Having been a featured speaker, award-winner, and expert in the field of customer retention, I knew this was an industry where I could be the best in the world for e-commerce clients internationally.

I caught a lucky break. COVID-19 gave me an advantage over everyone else: the world had accelerated into e-commerce overnight, providing me with a growing customer base that was highly interested in my services and expertise.

Fast forward to today, I now run HiFlyer Digital, a fast-growing email, SMS and CRM agency for e-commerce brands, manage a team of 8+ employees internationally, have a client roster of highly reputable 7, 8, 9, and 10-figure brands, and have a clear path forward for being the largest email, SMS and CRM agency in the world.

## What COVID-19 Taught Me

The point of this preface is as follows: COVID-19 was a catalyst for change. If you're an e-commerce brand, you know that customers pivoted to and away from you during the pandemic... but they haven't yet decided where to give their purchasing loyalty. The snowflakes - aka customers - are still landing, and the world is far from settled back into a normal routine.

Because customers are still in a state of indecisiveness, the pandemic is a once-in-a-lifetime opportunity to focus all your energy on building better customer relationships, personalizing the customer experience, and turning one-time buyers into lifetime buyers.

As you'll see from the market data and trends within this book, your customers are going to demand more and expect more from you post-pandemic. To make matters worse, Amazon, Meta, customer-centric apps, retail marketplaces (like Etsy), and Silicon Valley startups are positioning themselves to take more of your customers, market share, and profits. These well-funded players understand the snowglobe concept and are also seizing the once-in-a-lifetime COVID-19 opportunities.

It's time for the small yet scaling e-commerce business to win for a change. If I can pivot out of a pandemic and grow a marketing agency from scratch, your business can emerge stronger than ever. And I want YOU to win.

I want you to take advantage of the opportunities all around you, starting by building better customer relationships. If you create unbreakable bonds with your customers, your business will pivot from the pandemic stronger than ever before and compete to win with the top e-commerce brands in the world. The playing field will be completely leveled, and customers will stay loyal to you more than ever before.

In this book, I'm going to share the exact roadmap I use to build better customer relationships using email, SMS and CRM.

My goal is to level the playing field for small yet scaling e-commerce brands and help you compete and win at e-commerce.

***

*I believe in the power, uniqueness, and story of the small e-commerce business. For that reason, I'm on a mission to bring the secret strategies of the top 1% to small yet scaling e-commerce brands, leveling the playing field and helping them compete to win in a crowded e-commerce marketplace.*

**Isaac Hyman**

# CHAPTER ONE

## INTRODUCTION

**This book is your roadmap for building better customer relationships that yield immensely profitable, predictable, and sustainable revenue streams for your e-commerce business.**

**By the time you finish this book, you will learn the secret email, SMS and CRM playbooks of the top 1% and will be able to use them to create mind-blowing revenues for your business that turn one-time buyers into lifetime buyers.**

That may sound like a bold statement for brands who've given up on email and SMS or who think that settling for small email and SMS revenue streams is "normal."

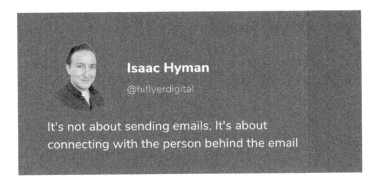

Isaac Hyman
@hiflyerdigital

It's not about sending emails. It's about connecting with the person behind the email

You'll quickly realize that this book goes beyond what you've typically thought about email marketing, workflows, marketing automations, or other email buzzwords.

This book doesn't really focus on the channel; in fact, when I meet a prospective client, I always say that we help build better customer relationships. We just happen to excel at doing it via email and SMS.

This book focuses on the person behind the email, which is all that matters. Building better customer relationships is not about the channel, the email address, or the phone number. It's about connecting with the person behind the email address. If you can connect with that customer on a 1:1 level, you'll yield more revenue instantly.

This book will illustrate the untapped customer value that exists within your email and SMS list while providing the exact game plan to extract that value consistently.

By internalizing this book's customer-centric philosophy and rolling out the strategy I'll share with you, you'll stop "sending emails" and start building relationships with the people behind the email and texts. The result: your customers will feel more connected to your brand and more willing to invest in a relationship with you.

## My Background & Story

To fully understand the power of great relationships, let me start with a personal story.

I was brought up as an adopted Colombian child in a pretty conservative home. Being adopted, I often felt the need to "measure up" to the other children and overcompensate for not being "natural" to my family. Kind of a sad way of looking at things, I know now, but I was a kid, and that's what I felt at the time. Back then, I felt different and looked different, so I craved every opportunity to blend in when possible.

Unfortunately, my adopted background wasn't the only difference I'd encounter. Life threw my family another challenge when my mother became blind when I was in grade school.

Back in the 80s, having a parent with a disability was not as acceptable as it is today; there was a stigma around disabilities, which caused a lot of self-doubt and anxiety in my upbringing.

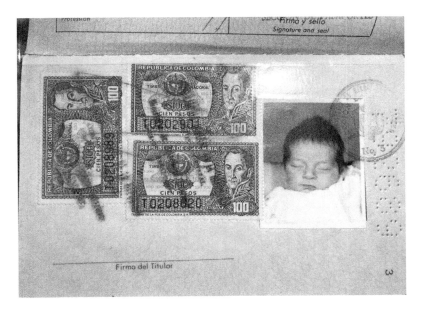

I struggled with being "normal" in front of the other kids. Being the kid with a blind parent, I was frustrated that I couldn't get rides to friends' homes or have family movie nights like the other kids.

While my friends played outdoor hockey and gathered for Sega Genesis playdates, my childhood memories were filled with moments of having to pitch in more than most. I had parental-like tasks like grocery shopping, cooking, trips to doctor's offices, expanded chores, and taking care of my siblings. I was the oldest child, so the responsibilities fell on me to care for the home while my Dad was working to make ends meet.

Because of my upbringing, I felt a need to overcompensate in the friendship department. My friendship goals were simple: be liked by everyone. I became extremely skilled at getting to the root of a person's mindset, likes, and dislikes and connecting with them in a deeply empathetic way.

I excelled in bonding with people by quickly finding our common denominator and accentuating that bond throughout the relationship.

Needless to say, being liked by everyone can be exhausting and not always rewarding. My teenage and college years were pretty much a 24/7 cocktail hour where I built a lot of great acquaintances and not many deep friendships.

Luckily for me, I met my wife, Olivia, and she's the greatest thing to ever happen to me. I credit her for refocusing my mindset and personality on deeper relationships rather than surface ones. Her love, attention, and encouragement is how I was able to break free from superficial relationships and explore deeper connections with the right people. Naturally, though, my bonding skills enabled me to become a highly successful salesperson.

I started my sales career in a high-intensity environment: door-to-door sales for an office supplies company.

As a college student at the time, that role was exciting, fast-paced, and rewarding for a personality like mine. It taught me how to pitch fast and close deals quickly. The downside of the role was that relationship building was non-existent; whenever I closed a new deal, I was on to the next one, never tasked with nurturing the sale into long-term clients.

I was like a combination of Michael Scott and Dwight Schrute rolled into one. I credit that job for helping me understand how to win over a customer, build a relationship instantly and close deals within minutes.

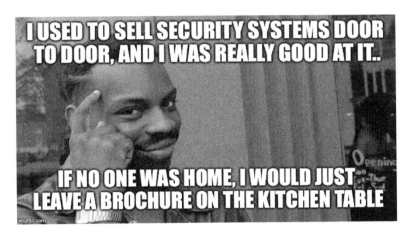

In fact, you can learn a lot by heading to the trenches in a business, talking to the gatekeepers, and swapping stories with the sales staff.

To this day, with every major brand I work with, I make it a point to dialogue with the sales team, customer service, and in-store personnel. The people on the front lines and in daily customer-facing roles can tell you a lot about the customers.

After my door-to-door sales role, I sought out a new role that focused on building relationships with every client, and that led me to digital ad sales for a regional media platform.

I managed about 150 clients with a regional advertising spend of $2M+ annually. Pivoting to consultative-based selling helped me understand the lifetime value of a great customer. I excelled in growing new clients spending $20,000 annually into powerhouse clients spending $300,000 annually. I also felt the sting of large clients reducing their local ad spend in favor of paid search and paid social. Understanding the care, attention, and education necessary to grow client value and reduce churn rates was critical to my eventual success in e-commerce.

## The Turning Point

After succeeding as a digital advertising account director, I opted to bring those skills to a new frontier: e-commerce. The field was growing fast, I was fascinated with the inner workings of the brands I shopped at, and I wanted to beef up my digital marketing skills. I posited that if I could develop a strong 1:1 sales relationship with a small network of Dream 100 clients, I could probably succeed at scaling those strategies digitally up to millions of e-commerce customers.

The approach was sound, but I learned that within the top 1% of e-commerce, there are a lot of stakeholders and processes.

It was great to join a well-known family of brands that prided itself on culture and product expertise, but it also meant that I'd have to table some of my customer-centric strategies in lieu of being more product-centric for a time.

In addition, while working at the number two retailer in the industry, I was always tasked and pressured with "keeping up" with the top brand in the industry. I struggled with convincing anyone that there was a better way than copycat marketing. With a high emphasis on copycatting our competitors, cumbersome marketing technology, and product-heavy emails, I wasn't sure my customer-centric philosophy would work here.

The first few months were a struggle, a tug-of-war between merchandising and marketing over who steered the marketing direction. Don't get me wrong: everyone on the team was phenomenally skilled and highly passionate. The challenge was in an overarching strategy - are we product-centric or customer-centric?

I quickly realized that in order to steer a big ship, I needed to take the approach one turn at a time; or, in email terms, one campaign at a time. Historically, their email revenue grew about

5-10% a year, driven primarily by product price increases or one-time new product announcements.

At the same time, the demands on my email team to keep up with the top dog led to late nights, long days, and burnt-out employees. After a few months, I considered moving on to the direct-to-consumer brands that were growing 10x as fast and had a true customer-centric approach to their marketing.

## The Breakthrough

My perspective changed a couple months later. Almost sensing the overarching direction wasn't where they should be, the company ownership brought in a fresh CEO and CMO who were entirely customer-centric in their approach to e-commerce. These two visionaries would eventually give me the trust and blessing to help implement their vision through email, SMS and CRM.

I put forward my strategy - which I now call my S.P.A.M. strategy, as you'll learn later in this book! - and refocused all our technologies, campaign planning, automations, and testing around the customer. I treated my email team of five and one reporting agency as a startup, complete with a unique mission, vision, and values statement that revolves everything around the customer. I even use those values today at HiFlyer Digital; specifically, the "customer flywheel" approach (hence the name HiFlyer) pioneered by Jim Collins, author of *Good to Great*.

Combining customer segmentation with data-driven personalization, I was able to drive a 50% increase in revenue year over year... while mailing 40% less overall, reducing our email footprint and unsubscribe rates as a bonus. I give full credit to the email team for the success; my strategy was only as good as the execution of the team. After all, one of our core values was "work smart, not hard," so the team was more than happy to focus on hitting our revenue goals in half the time!

Here's one of our best years as an example. In 2018, I had already beat 2017's email & SMS revenue numbers by mid-August - which surpassed the mid 8-figure channel revenue range - solidifying our channel as the fastest-growing, most profitable channel in the company.

ANNUAL RESULTS | KEY VALUES

—

**50% GROWTH**
IN EMAIL
REVENUE

**40% DROP**
IN EMAILS
DELIVERED

**20% INCREASE**
IN ACTIVE
CUSTOMERS

It went beyond dollars and cents, though; the merchandisers also realized that a product-centric or copycat approach was less effective than a customer-centric approach when it comes to email & SMS. That buy-in helped marketing and merchandising work collaboratively on unique customer strategies, promotions, and products that exist to this day.

Everything was going well for the company. Maybe too well, in fact. Company leadership struck while the iron was hot; when the CEO and CMO ended up taking leadership roles at larger e-commerce brands, I created an exit strategy for myself.

**Isaac Hyman**

Award-Winning E-Commerce Email, SMS & CRM Marketer,
Speaker & Co-Founder | Over 2 Billion Emails/SMS Sent and
$300M Revenue Generated for 7, 8 and 9 Figure Brands

Talks about #crm, #ecommerce, #smsmarketing, #digitalagency, and
#emailmarketing

New York City Metropolitan Area · Contact info

2,277 followers · 500+ connections

HiFlyer Digital

Yeshiva University

I took the time to build e-commerce, vendor, and industry relationships that are still strong today. I booked speaking engagements at nationwide e-commerce conferences and created an agency go-to-market plan in my spare time.

Because I'm a visionary type of guy, I had already created a successful side hustle to help the transition into agency life when the time was right. My wife and I agreed that when the kids were grown up, and we saw an opportunity, we would seize it.

There's no bigger sign that the time was right than a pandemic. COVID-19 hit a year later, and I was fully prepared to exit the company stronger than when I came in.

They say luck favors the prepared. COVID-19 turned e-commerce into the fastest growing channel so I seized the opportunity to go all-in on my agency.

Going full-time into agency life during the most tumultuous period of our lifetime was extremely nerve-wracking. But the decision was a long time coming. COVID-19 presented that opportunity, and I never looked back. Within three months of leaving my role as Director of Email & CRM, I had replaced my comfy six-figure compensation. Within six months, I doubled it.

When CRM became the hottest e-commerce job on the market at the beginning of 2021 - an influx of one-time COVID-19 e-commerce customers required a strategy to turn them into lifetime buyers after all - I turned down multiple mid-six-figure job offers and trendy titles from billion-dollar retailers and direct-to-consumer brands.

Rejecting a comfortable compensation was a hard thing for me to do. I naturally craved the comfort and stability of a J-O-B, but thanks to the encouragement of my wife and family, I was determined to set my own comfort level.

I took the agency to the next level by partnering with an operations and martech expert, Yaakov Rosenberg, and 2021 scaled up even faster than 2020.

We rebranded as HiFlyer Digital and focused everything on our core competency of building better customer relationships for e-commerce brands.

I even partnered with an agency accelerator, Seven Figure Agency with Josh Nelson, and we were locked and loaded with our agency fundamentals, roadmap, and goals.

Fast forward to today, we now run a highly profitable e-commerce agency that focuses on email, SMS and CRM, with a staff of 8 globally managing a client roster that contains 7, 8, 9-figure, and even billion-dollar brands.

This book is primarily about the power of your customer and how e-commerce brands can tap into the true buying power of every customer simply by building a relationship with them using email, SMS and CRM.

But if there is one secondary message about my journey I'd like to leave you with, it would be that small business owners can be more powerful than the largest Fortune 500 e-commerce conglomerate.

The only reason I exist is to help level the playing field for the underdog. With 68% of U.S. e-commerce sales belonging to just

10 national retailers, the small business needs help to compete and win in a very crowded marketplace. I'm proud to say that we're here to help you win.

## The Lessons

There's a reason I'm sharing my background with you. If you take one thing away from my story, let it be this: If I, as a true underdog, could build a fast-growing agency from scratch during the most challenging years of our lifetime, acquire billion-dollar brands as clients, and grow their email and SMS revenues by 200% to 300%, your e-commerce business can flourish as well.

The same tools that exist for the top 1% are available to you; it just requires a strategic direction, an outsider point of view, and a passion for building customer relationships.

**As a big fan of Simon Sinek's TED Talk, *The Power of Why*, I can confidently say that our WHY is to help brands like yours build better customer relationships.** Everything we do is about building better relationships and getting to know the person behind the 1s, 0s, emails, and texts. We exist to create stronger connections in an often-disconnected digital world.

We just happen to do it best by focusing on segmentation and personalization with email, SMS and CRM. That's our HOW and

WHAT. But even if those channels die down a decade from now, having a WHY will enable both our business and clients to adapt to new channels, initiatives, and technologies.

I've searched the space already, and I'm literally the only email, SMS and CRM agency owner who actually wrote a book for small business owners like you… and that's because I want you to win.

I'm also the only agency owner who's sat on your side of the table. As a Director of CRM at the top 1%, I've personally hired and fired agencies, reported results to bosses and ownership, been burned by agency work and bad results, and challenged with getting buy-in from different departments and stakeholders. I've had to fast-track certain customer-centric initiatives and table passion projects, all for the sake of the business.

As a customer-centric marketer, I've butted heads with product-centric teams who believe product is the tip of the spear. I've had to battle against changing our entire marketing strategy for the sake of one customer complaint (out of millions of customers).

Whether you're an owner, CEO, CMO, Director, Manager, or Associate, I know the challenges you face because I've sat in your seat. And because I've walked in your shoes, all the strategies, tactics, and advice I share in this book will help you achieve the respect, buy-in, and goals you're looking to reach from a customer-centric marketing approach.

I hope this book and my story will help you overcome any hurdles and remind you that the magic of email and SMS is not in the size of your brand or the size of your list; what matters is the relationship you have with your list, and the relationship customers have with your brand.

## Who Is This Book For?

My legacy marketing agency used to get hired by hundreds of diverse brands in multiple different niches with different strategy requirements. From SaaS to non-profits, book authors, to restaurants, all of them need email, SMS and CRM services. The demand may have been good for my wallet but trying to succeed in every niche is a client retention disaster.

Having learned from the past, HiFlyer Digital is fully zeroed in on our core niche and Dream 100 prospect.

Yet even when we niched down into the e-commerce space, we faced additional challenges, such as sub-niche specialization like outdoor & sporting goods, retail clients or direct-to-consumer (D2C) brands. On top of that, our agency focuses on brands that are in scale-up mode (as opposed to startups) and have shown a propensity to invest in marketing.

Identifying who we can help the most is what makes running a marketing agency quite challenging.. With that in mind, this chapter is exactly about identifying who will benefit the most from this book.

Although we've found our core e-commerce niche, this book can help numerous types of e-commerce businesses, markets, and personas.

Based on the success we've had with all types of e-com clients, I've identified a few personas that would truly benefit from this book. They include:

**1. E-commerce brands trying to scale & grab market share.**

If growth is not something you're interested in, you probably won't invest as much energy into growing customer lifetime value. E-commerce success boils down to two strategies: acquisition and retention. Email & SMS covers your retention and helps grow customers into loyalists, but you must invest in an acquisition strategy to get that customer in the first place. Growth necessitates growth.

**2. Business owners who pivoted to e-commerce during the pandemic but haven't "figured it out yet."**

The brands that pivoted to e-commerce during the pandemic are the second most common type of shops we encounter. Most stores, retailers, and brands didn't truly think much of e-commerce until COVID-19 demanded it. Now, these brands realize e-commerce is here to stay and need to invest more into the success of their online operation.

**3. E-commerce shops looking to break free from Amazon and create a D2C position.**

We'll discuss this in more depth later. Overall, breaking free from reliance on Amazon or other marketplaces - or reliance on paid media on Google and Facebook, as well - is going to be a continued trend.

There's a ceiling to how large a brand can grow - in size and in profits - within an Amazon, Etsy, or eBay marketplace, and brands are seeing that with every painful fee increase or frustrating platform change.

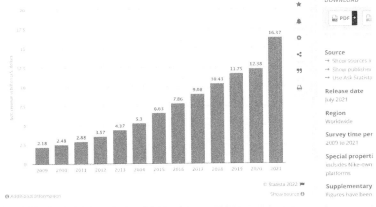

Retail & Trade › Fashion & Accessories
**Nike brand's direct-to-consumer revenue worldwide from 2009 to 2021**
*(in billion U.S. dollars)*

Take Nike; they ran an Amazon pilot and eventually canceled it at the end of 2019 in order to pursue a stronger D2C strategy. The strategy has paid off very well, and Nike saw a 39% year-over-year growth in 2021.

**4. Retailers who want to establish a competitive advantage in front of their customers.**

Ever shopped in a store, found the perfect item, and then price-compared it on Amazon while you're in the store? You're far from alone. Competing on price is a race to the bottom, especially if you're not Amazon. As such, retailers need to create distinctive competitive advantages to keep customers coming back, such as enhanced customer value, product expertise, or unique education. Email, SMS and CRM are the perfect tools for creating that unique value in the minds of customers.

**5. Direct-to-consumer (D2C) brands who are looking to stand out from the ever-growing list of brands in their space.**

Similar to the marketplace challenge, the number of direct-to-consumer brands is growing quite fast, funded by Silicon Valley venture capitalists. Take the mattress industry: in 2010, there were about 20 D2C mattress brands, yet, in 2021, there were upwards of 175 competitors, according to CNBC.

Simply going D2C is not a recipe for success anymore; developing a unique brand story, mission, and value proposition within a customer-centric channel like email & SMS becomes even more critical.

**6. Digitally-native e-commerce brands who want to ensure customer loyalty in a fickle marketplace.**

You've heard about my snowglobe analogy already, but McKinsey actually summarizes the customer loyalty issue even better: consumer loyalty has been shaken up as 76% of customers have changed stores, brands, or the way they shop during the pandemic. Digitally native brands are not immune to fickle customer loyalty, and the pandemic proved it. Excelling at building better customer experiences and relationships is the only way to ensure loyalty after the pandemic.

In summary, this book is for e-commerce brands who really want to build better customer relationships that lead to profitable, predictable, and sustainable revenue. From scale-up to startup, unicorn to the top 1%, if you feel the customer is everything to your business, this book will help.

With 84% of customers craving personalization yet only 15% of brands actually achieving that goal, I can confidently say that this book will resonate with brands who want to bridge that gap and create unbreakable relationships that will weather any challenge, competition, or downturn.

## I've Been in Your Shoes

A few years ago, when I was vetting a few ESPs to determine which vendor would be the best for our business, I was enamored with client success stories from their sales reps (SDRs) of how Sephora, Wayfair, Nike, and other brands were creating uber-personalization strategies using their ESP / CRM / CDP platforms.

Needless to say, I was jealous. The brands I represented were pretty robust as well, doing multi-millions in revenue every year with eight-figure email lists and growing.

My ego got the better of me. I should be up there with those brands and sharing my insights with everyone! I figured that the best path forward was to embrace the exact technologies the top brands used and immediately reap the benefits for the companies I worked with and for my own personal branding success.

What I learned fast - and, in some cases, painfully - was that technology is merely a tool. I needed to be the one who wielded that tool like Thor from Avengers Infinity War (remember that "Bring Me Thanos!" scene? One of my favorite scenes ever!). If I didn't embrace a new marketing strategy, no tool would miraculously get me to a new level.

When I first had the opportunity to shape our email & SMS team, technology, and strategy in the way I envisioned, it all clicked from there. I turned a former product-centric, merchant-driven marketing channel into a fully customer-centric, data-driven, automated marketing powerhouse.

I led a team that grew email & SMS revenues by 50% while reducing send volumes by 40% using the exact strategy I'll show you in this book. But it wasn't just because of the tech or the timing; it was because our team as a whole changed our mindset.

And the technology came through for me anyway! A year later, my team and I were honored with the "Best Email Performer" Award at Bluecore Summit, beating out Sephora, Jockey, and other billion-dollar brands.

What's the message here? Changing your mindset is the key part. If anyone tells you you're just one piece of technology, one plugin, one app, or one creative away from greatness, don't believe them. Changing your mindset is all that matters.

The top brands spend millions onboarding new technologies every year... only to use 10% of the tech's full potential and pivot to hotter tech a year later. Plugins come and go, and technologies get gobbled up by bigger firms. Technology, though nice to have, is not a strategy.

In fact, that's one of HiFlyer Digital's strong suits; whereas most email & SMS agencies excel only in Klaviyo, we excel in Klaviyo and dozens of other ESPs because our strategy is ESP-agnostic, not ESP-dependent. And having personally implemented or kicked the tires on nearly every ESP, I can tell you that the right ESP is critical.

But changing the mindset is the most important part. Shifting into a customer-centric mindset will grow your business faster than any tool, tech, team, or tactic.

There's another takeaway here that you should know: I've been in the trenches with you. If you're a marketer for a top e-commerce brand, I've sat in the same seat as you and been tasked to drive more dollars and send fewer emails.

If you're a business owner, I've actually hired and fired agencies as well, and I know the feeling of "being burned." That's why I always say to the brands who hire me: I've actually been there and done that, talked the talk and walked the walk, and I will tell you what's true, what's false, what's important, and what's not.

That experience and trust have helped me land speaking engagements at eTail West, Etail East, Optimove's Post-Funnel, and other events, where I share proven strategies for building better customer relationships and humanizing your marketing.

Those events continue to be such great experiences because I personally connect with brands at all levels and build lifelong friendships with people, vendors, and tech. Being on the brand side allows me to demo the latest technologies and create the ultimate marketing tech stack for my clients.

**But to summarize my background, lessons, and philosophy into one core message: I've sat in your shoes, actually done the work, and I want to help you succeed at e-commerce as well as I have.**

As a small-business owner who has walked in your shoes, I always remind myself about a core tenet of customer relationships: **no one cares about what I know until they know how much I care.** I could be the smartest guy in the room and feel comfortable pitching C-level executives for the top e-commerce brands; none of that matters unless I show how much I care about the brand, mission, and customers.

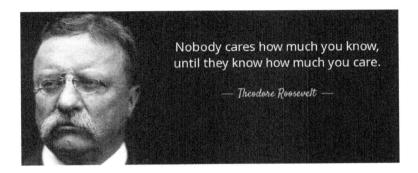

Nobody cares how much you know, until they know how much you care.

— Theodore Roosevelt —

And that's the best takeaway from this chapter: the more you show you care about your customers, the more they'll spend with you.

Email, SMS and CRM are just tools to help you show caring, empathy, and attention. It's no surprise that lack of care, lack of attention, or perceived indifference are the number one reasons customers leave your business.

I care about the success of your small business, and it pains me when I hear stories like the one I'm about to share in the next chapter. I took months to write this book because I want you to succeed, scale and win at e-commerce.

Now that you know that I care about your success - in fact, my whole agency depends on the success of e-commerce brands like yours! - it's time to understand if customers care about you.

So, it's only fitting that we start this book on building better customer relationships by focusing on the top reasons why customers will leave you this year.

# CHAPTER TWO

## THE STATE OF E-COMMERCE

My client was nearly in tears. I don't usually leave a client crying after a meeting, so, rest assured, this wasn't my doing.

For forty-five minutes of our scheduled lunch meeting, this prospect, a successful business owner with five locations and an e-commerce store doing over $20M a year in revenue, was complaining about Brooklinen.

We all know Brooklinen. It's one of the darlings of the direct-to-consumer marketplace (D2C).

They've grown from $50M annually to over $600M in four years, charming customers with their comfortable linens, fantastic reviews, and customer-centric approach.

But my customer was not a raving fan. All I heard for forty-five minutes was grumbling about how Brooklinen's quality was inferior, posturing about how his brand has been in business for 30 years, and questioning why customers would even consider shopping at a tech-funded startup!

He was clearly upset but, more pressingly, kind of hurt. He felt left behind by the industry, shifting consumer shopping habits, and even his own customers. A four-year-old well-funded linen startup was heavily competing with his local business that took 30 years to scale. And he was hurt, confused, and angry all at the same time.

This is just one story of thousands that aren't being shared with the public too often.

It's the David and Goliath tale for the 21st century: small yet stable, hard-working, and long-lasting businesses are being quickly surpassed by venture-funded startups in the digitally-native world of e-commerce.

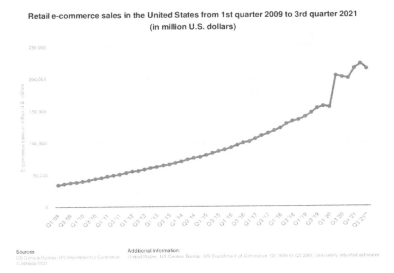

Retail e-commerce sales in the United States from 1st quarter 2009 to 3rd quarter 2021 (in million U.S. dollars)

Don't get me wrong; I love everything about Brooklinen, Amazon, Glossier, and every customer-centric e-commerce brand out there. As a consumer, they offer great convenience, competitive pricing, and fast fulfillment. What's not to love?

But this story is a cautionary tale: e-commerce is growing really fast - experts say e-commerce accelerated by three years in just the first six months of the pandemic - and if your brand isn't keeping pace, you'll be left behind.

Ironically, small brands have the same tools to help compete against the big brands, yet most don't understand where to focus their energy nor how to remain competitive in an ever-changing marketplace.

Eventually, brands like my prospective client are caught blindsided by new technology, changing shopping habits, and even customer churn. These businesses could prevent being blindsided by understanding how the top 1% of e-commerce brands operate, putting a strategy in place to level the playing fields, and then focusing all their efforts on the customer experience and retention.

Let's talk about Glossier. With only 79 products in their catalog, Glossier, a makeup and beauty brand founded by Emily Weiss, crossed the $100M revenue mark in 2018. The VC-backed company, with $86M in funding, employs 200 full-time employees across three offices yet only has two physical stores (Recently, Glossier's brand stumbled due to a lack of diversity, but the speed at which they scaled is the main takeaway here).

With the shift to global online sales, a human-to-brand connection was quite lacking, and Emily cleverly jumped in that gap. She envisioned a brand that was inspired by real life, just like her blog, and where the customer was not the end but the starting point.

From the beginning, Glossier has been a D2C brand, owning its entire sales funnel and customer experience. This gives them incredible power and controls their data and destiny. Brands like Glossier are popping up and challenging legacy brands and retailers everywhere.

Casper, the D2C mattress company that launched in 2014, went from unprofitable to $750 million in four years by utilizing a customer-centric business approach. They examined the pain points of purchasing a mattress—driving to the store, dealing with an aggressive salesperson, choosing between dozens of different options—and set out to solve those pain points for the consumer.

Casper's customer-centric approach has enabled them to grow exponentially because consumers are looking for a brand that puts them at the center of the buying experience. To this day, they've remained dedicated to their customer-centric values since the beginning, offering a money-back guarantee for any customer that isn't completely satisfied with their purchase.

Customer-centric brands like Casper, Brooklinen, and Glossier are leaders in the e-commerce market because they're dedicated to understanding and satisfying every need of the customer. Everything they do revolves around the customer, and I'll explain that in more depth later in this chapter.

Focusing on the customer is essential to creating a great user experience for your online store and establishing a lasting connection with users that transcends just dollars and cents. All these D2C brands are positioning themselves to compete with you, acquire your customers and win their loyalty. And we haven't even mentioned Amazon yet, the pace-setter when it comes to e-commerce.

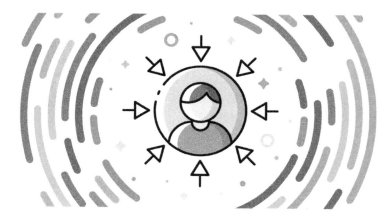

Overall, the state of e-commerce today is quite challenging for small businesses. Remember the snowglobe: we're in the midst of an unfinished point in history where customers haven't yet landed on their preferred long-term brands. You still have time to level the playing field in your favor. In order to level the playing field, we must first understand why customers leave your brand for the other competitors, stores, and startups.

So, let's dive into the top seven reasons why customers will abandon your brand for Amazon and your competitors this year. After that, I'll show you how to prevent it.

**Webinar: 7 Reasons Customers Leave You**

For those who are video lovers, this chapter was condensed into a 45-minute webinar that you can watch on-demand for free. Simply go to HiFlyerDigital.com/sevenreasons or scan the QR code below, and you'll be able to watch the full webinar on-demand. Studies show, though, that reading and listening help increase the chances of retaining the information, so be sure to read on!

# 7 Reasons Why Customers Will Leave You

## Reason 1. Amazon's Scale

Amazon's scale is bigger than ever, and its sheer size is attracting your customers first. Look at the graph below:

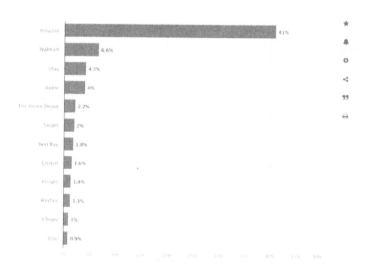

41% of total U.S. e-commerce sales in 2020 are attributed to Amazon. The top nine brands directly under Amazon attribute only 26% of total e-commerce revenue; Amazon's revenue is bigger than those brands combined. In addition, Amazon is projected to hit 50% by the end of 2022. With size, scale, and selection like that, Amazon pretty much controls the pace of e-commerce.

For brands that sell on Amazon, size is a huge benefit from a shopper's point of view, but it has limited promise from a growth perspective. Amazon is considered a walled garden and is hoarding valuable customer data from the brands they support. The data that Amazon does share isn't highly qualitative or super-actionable. So, you're kind of stuck either playing with Amazon or not playing at all.

Net revenue of Amazon from 1st quarter 2007 to 3rd quarter 2021
*(in billion U.S. dollars)*

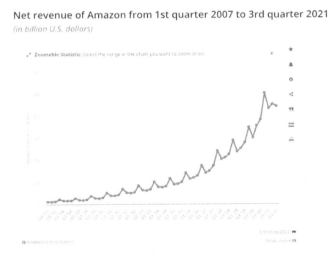

Brands that are struggling to compete with Amazon's scale have one advantage. Since Amazon has a huge scale, the shopping experience is commonly referred to as a faceless commerce experience. Customers don't really talk to someone on Amazon, get to know customer service, or build a relationship for product adoption. Strong brand story-telling and creating a "brand-face" will be an opportunity we'll go into shortly

Because of their scale, Amazon will continue to command better pricing; combined with their leadership in logistics, value, and fulfillment, your margins and unique selling proposition (USP) will be heavily impacted.

But there's more bad news: their next milestone is brick and mortar. They're going to come to a local store near you and compete for last-mile fulfillment.

When customers have a need to fill, Amazon's scale advantage earns them a first pass over the smaller brands simply because customers can literally find everything on Amazon. In short, Amazon's scale attracts your customers first. They come for the selection and scale, and they'll stay for everything else.

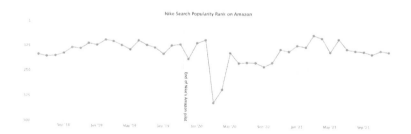

Nike Search Popularity Rank on Amazon

## Reason 2. The Search Monopoly

Big fan of Nike? There was a time when Nike was listed on Amazon. Nike ran a pilot on Amazon to determine platform viability, but around the end of 2019, Nike opted to delist, simply preferring to go direct-to-consumer.

The above graph reflects the search trends for Nike products throughout 2020. Notice a trend? Even after Nike delisted in 2019, their brand still experienced a steady volume of product searches throughout 2020.

Aside from one little dip in March 2020 - when everyone was searching for COVID-19 masks, sanitizers, and the like - Amazon was the go-to search platform for millions of customers seeking Nike shoes and apparel.

Currently, 78% of product searches start on Amazon, not Google. This statistic essentially turns Amazon into the largest shopping search engine, dwarfing Google's monopoly. As evidenced by Nike, even if your products aren't selling on Amazon, people are still searching there. Searches for "Nike sneakers," "Nike apparel," or "Nike leggings" and on all start on Amazon... not on Google.

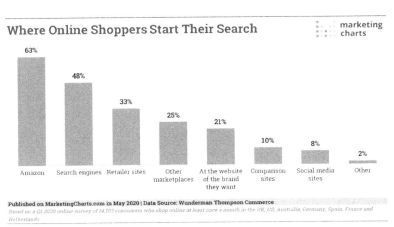

**Where Online Shoppers Start Their Search**

marketing charts

Published on MarketingCharts.com in May 2020 | Data Source: Wunderman Thompson Commerce
Based on a Q1 2020 online survey of 14,103 consumers who shop online at least once a month in the UK, US, Australia, Germany, Spain, France and Netherlands

Remember the in-store shopping experience we discussed earlier? Let's recap it here: how many times have you been in a store and started searching on Amazon for similar or exact products as what you have in your hand, researching if you can get a better deal, faster delivery, greater size selection, or better value?

We all do that… and it's because Amazon has become a search engine for our products and shopping preferences. Google has become a search for "how to" and topical searches. As shown below, Amazon wins on headphone searches, but Google wins on the gaming-related searches (such as how to game, popular games, or gaming stores near me.)

For Google, it gets even worse. Amazon has the highest organic search market share for all apparel, fashion, and health and beauty searches, ranking number one across the board for multiple categories.

That means, even on Google, Amazon owns the search for the most popular categories. And I haven't even discussed their annual ad budget for paid search yet.

Owning product search is yet another first-mover advantage for Amazon; it affords them the opportunity to own the customer experience at the very start of a product search.

Owning the selection, search, and scale of the shopping experience is how Amazon steals away your customers.

## Reason 3. Amazon's Conglomerate of Value.

We've established that Amazon owns scale and search; those reasons alone mean that Amazon is nearly unstoppable when it comes to gaining new customers and keeping them reliant on their ecosystem. Amazon's huge conglomerate value, though, is instrumental in breaking customers from their loyalty to other brands and retaining the customers they gain. The sheer amount of value add-ons is nearly unbeatable.

**Number of Amazon Prime users (US) from 2017 to 2022 (Statista)**

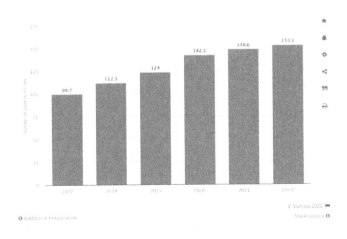

The Statista graph shows the annual growth of Amazon Prime users. Although growth has slowed in recent years, Prime membership is almost table stakes for being an Amazon customer. Everyone has Prime and are leveraging Prime value in numerous ways.

In 2017, Amazon Prime membership was about 100 million; currently, Prime membership is projected to grow to 153 million subscribers in 2022. Amazon Prime membership makes financial sense because of the value-stacking that comes with Prime. Amazon Prime offers customers great benefits such as free two-day delivery, special grocery deals at Whole Foods, Amazon Prime Video access, Audible access, and numerous other benefits across their portfolio of brands and services.

That Amazon Prime value-stacking is simply unbeatable and extremely convenient as membership can be managed seamlessly across brands, services, and apps, all from one Prime account. You log in to one account, and you now have Prime advantage across multiple platforms - Audible, Amazon Prime, Amazon Cloud Player, Whole Foods, Zappos, and on and on. As of the time of writing this book, Amazon recently launched "Buy Now with Amazon Prime" on multiple retailer websites, offering another value proposition that brands have to compete with.

Amazon was the first to pioneer a one-click checkout, so it's no surprise that customers have a one-click option for unlocking immense value.

Unless you're one of the top ten e-commerce brands, creating a conglomerate of value to rival Amazon Prime is simply not feasible for the small guy. The value of an Amazon Prime membership is reason number three why customers leave you for Amazon.

# Reason 4. The Flywheel's Dominance

Most brands understand the concept of a funnel. You drive qualified traffic to a landing page or lead magnet, capture the visitor data and nurture that lead into a customer.

For e-commerce brands, though, the funnel is about as useful as a sieve. Acquiring a one-time customer is relatively easy compared to keeping a customer loyal and gaining multiple purchases. In fact, 74% of e-commerce customers remain one-time buyers, so the funnel only serves to attract low-profit, discount-hunting customers.

The flywheel is the better approach for creating profitable, predictable, and sustainable e-commerce growth. In the book, *Good to Great,* by Jim Collins, the flywheel acts as a constant source of acquiring, converting, and retaining customers, all on the power of its own momentum. And that flywheel concept - which I highly recommend you study up on! - is reason number four for why customers leave you: Amazon's flywheel.

Currently, Amazon sets the pace on logistics and selection for customers. And we've already established that Amazon is the leader in scale and search. But what does it look like when you piece all those advantages together? Take a good look at the Amazon flywheel.

Take the flow step-by-step. Amazon focused everything on customer experience and superior software. Jeff Bezos reasoned that if the customer experience, product selection, and ease of checkout were simple, intuitive, and personalized, customers would come back. That's the second stage: traffic. The better the experience, the more traffic to the website.

With more traffic to the website, Amazon became more popular, which was attractive to book publishers at the time who saw an opportunity to sell more books, accessories, and magazines. The number of sellers grew, which led to higher selection.

And not just a large selection but also, due to the power of Amazon's technology, a curated selection of products personalized to the customer. Personalization leads to a better customer experience, which leads to more traffic. More traffic leads to even more sellers, new product categories, and new revenue streams, which is the definition of more selection. Amazon created the perfect e-commerce flywheel that's running on its own momentum.

Incidentally, their flywheel was so good that Amazon was able to create a separate business unit focused on selling their own technology to other brands looking to scale their business.

That business unit is now known as Amazon Web Services. AWS owns 33% of the cloud computing market, and it's on track to hit $71 billion in annual revenue on 40% annual growth.

According to McKinsey, 75% of e-commerce brands made two-day delivery a priority in 2021, and 42% made same-day delivery a priority this year in 2022. Amazon launched free two-day delivery with Prime membership back in 2005, 15 years ahead of everyone else! Let that number sink in - 3 out of 4 brands are trying to make two-day delivery a priority, not even a guarantee. True to form, while brands are struggling to play catch-up, Amazon already launched one-day delivery in 2019.

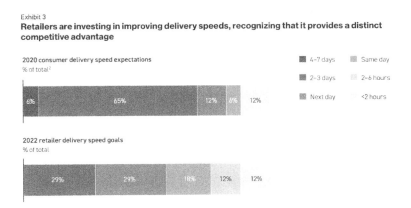

Exhibit 3
**Retailers are investing in improving delivery speeds, recognizing that it provides a distinct competitive advantage**

2020 consumer delivery speed expectations
% of total[2]

| ■ 4-7 days | ▨ Same day |
| ■ 2-3 days | 2-6 hours |
| ■ Next day | <2 hours |

6% | 65% | 12% | 6% | 12%

2022 retailer delivery speed goals
% of total

29% | 29% | 18% | 12% | 12%

Amazon is simply more convenient than you, and the ultimate form of customer loyalty within e-commerce is convenience. Amazon will deliver to you in two days, then one day, then two hours for Prime Grocery, then one hour in certain areas, and, shortly, brick and mortar in-store pickup. The barrier to competing with Amazon's dominant flywheel is too high.

Let's recap where Amazon is. They have the scale and selection, they get first-pass by being the default search engine for shoppers, they can fulfill faster, cheaper, and more efficiently than anyone, and they value-stack every order with great add-ons. That entire flywheel is why your customers leave for Amazon.

So, for brands that aren't named Amazon, what's the alternative? Throw our hands up in the air and give in? No, you have plenty of options, and here's one of the more popular ones: pair with a technology that can meet your customer where they are. If customers expect an "Amazon-like" experience everywhere they shop, you'll need to partner with the right apps, tech, and vendors to meet that customer where they are.

Meeting a customer where they are allows e-commerce brands to deliver on customer expectations on selection, fulfillment, service, and experience. For most brands, that means getting a better technology partner. For example, if a restaurant doesn't have a mobile-friendly, easy-to-navigate website, online menu, or easy ordering experience, they can partner with DoorDash, UberEats, or Seamless to create the experience customers demand.

Those apps and technologies will certainly help level the playing fields to a degree, but, as you'll learn next, that partnership comes with a major challenge to your customers and bottom line.

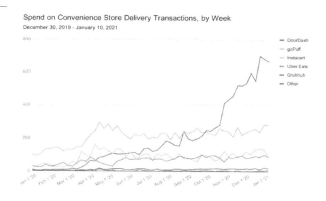

Spend on Convenience Store Delivery Transactions, by Week
December 30, 2019 - January 10, 2021

## Reason 5. Meet the Tech Middlemen

For the previous four reasons, we dove into Amazon's immense value, selection, scale, and flywheel. Whether you're able to compete or not with all those hurdles, we can certainly agree with one thing: customers love the Amazon experience. So, it's no surprise that customers prefer to shop at brands that can best replicate the Amazon experience. Which companies are best-positioned to replicate that digitally-native experience? Silicon Valley startups, apps, and social media.

If you want to level the playing field when it comes to customer experience, pair with an app or technology that can match and even outperform Amazon's app and experience.

If you've paired yourself with great technology, you're not alone. DoorDash, a restaurant ordering app, and Instacart, a grocery shopping and delivery app, are growing by 25% year over year.

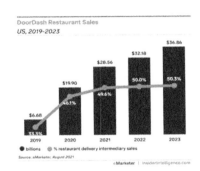

DoorDash Restaurant Sales
US, 2019-2023

Why are these brands growing so fast? Their reasoning can be summarized like this: "We're going to make buying your favorite groceries or buying your favorite restaurant meals super-easy with a user-friendly app, huge selection of restaurants, order tracking, and fast delivery!" Sounds great! Essentially, they're replicating the Amazon experience for their industry.

Another example that may be more relevant for e-commerce brands is ShopRunner. ShopRunner, a membership service for shoppers that was recently acquired by FedEx, promised free two-day delivery and free returns for thousands of e-commerce brands. If your brand partnered with ShopRunner and the customer signed up for ShopRunner, presto! Two-day delivery and free returns on your order were guaranteed.

Here's the problem. You've enabled an app to become a middleman between you and your customer. These apps fuel their growth by owning customer data, which helps them maintain customer loyalty, predict churn, and create better acquisition strategies. Apps positioning themselves between you and your customer is key to their growth strategy, and here's the end result: your customers become loyal TO THE APP, not you.

Think beyond the immediate sale you may gain from the app you onboarded. Go further back to Amazon's flywheel also. DoorDash has the users, and they have the selection of restaurants.

At any point, DoorDash could change their app to give preferential treatment to advertisers or higher-paying restaurant chains. DoorDash could demand a premium from you or place you towards the bottom of their search engine. A small restaurant has nowhere to turn: a ton of customers come from DoorDash, and businesses can't turn their back on that revenue stream. You're in a major quandary now.

In these scenarios, you need to pick your poison. Enabling a technology that you don't own to help you meet customers where they expect to be met and replicate the Amazon experience will lead to two trade-offs: trade away customer data or trade away profit margin.

In some cases, you may be trading away both. Customers will end up being loyal to the app's experience and convenience instead of loyal to your brand.

And if a competitor has the same app, you have no competitive advantage. That's reason number five why customers will leave you this year; loyalty to the app experience and not to you.

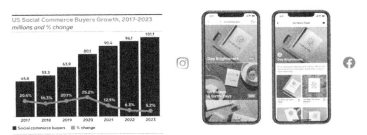

We've dived into the app and tech side of things. Now let's talk about the social media angle, namely Meta. We all know Meta by their other brands: Facebook, Instagram, and WhatsApp. These brands are no stranger to e-commerce; social commerce is growing fast, projected to rise double digits through 2023.

Although the vast majority haven't used social media to purchase products, COVID-19 expedited a transformation in buying habits. With Instagram Shop, Facebook Shop, and WhatsApp acting as a key customer service option, it will only be a matter of time before Meta becomes a key player in e-commerce.

Of course, selling on Meta means sacrificing a slice from your profit pie. If paid social wasn't already driving down your margins, selling on Facebook will certainly not help you become more profitable.

Worse, Meta has little incentive to share more data points with you if it means you'll spend less on ads or take customers away from their ecosystem.

Want proof? This woman's handle on Instagram was @Metaverse. According to The New York Times, when Facebook changed its name to Meta, her account was instantly disabled for "pretending to be someone else." Here's an excerpt from The New York Times article:

The New York Times

*Her Instagram Handle Was 'Metaverse.' Last Month, It Vanished.*

Five days after Facebook changed its name to Meta, an Australian artist found herself blocked, with seemingly no recourse, from an account documenting nearly a decade of her life and work.

*In October, Thea-Mai Baumann, an Australian artist and technologist, found herself sitting on prime internet real estate.*

*In 2012, she had started an Instagram account with the handle @metaverse, a name she used in her creative work. On the account, she documented her life in Brisbane, where she studied fine art, and her travels to Shanghai, where she built an augmented reality company called Metaverse Makeovers.*

*She had fewer than 1,000 followers when Facebook, the parent company of Instagram, announced on Oct. 28 that it was changing its name. Henceforth, Facebook would be known as Meta, a reflection of its focus on the metaverse, a virtual world it sees as the future of the internet.*

*In the days before, as word leaked out, Ms. Baumann began receiving messages from strangers offering to buy her Instagram handle. "You are now a millionaire," one person wrote on her account. Another warned: "fb isn't gonna buy it, they're gonna take it."*

*On Nov. 2, exactly that happened. Early that morning, when she tried to log in to Instagram, she found that the account had been disabled. A message on the screen read: "Your account has been blocked for pretending to be someone else."*

What's the moral here? You and millions of brands are just renting data from Meta, leasing space to create posts and stories that get likes, comments, and shares. With one algorithm change or shift in strategy, your presence on Meta can be changed or deleted for good. And Meta has done this before; remember when Instagram deleted fake followers or when Facebook deprioritized organic business page posts over friend posts? History is not on your side.

The point is this: Meta is in a fantastic position to capture some of your sales and take a piece of your revenue pie away from you. As mentioned above, customers will become more loyal to the app, to the platform, to the social medium, instead of you.

Placing apps, technologies, or brands in between you and the customer is a guaranteed way to lose customer loyalty. That loyalty may erode quickly or slowly, but it will erode. That's reason number five for why brands are losing customers.

## Reason 6. The Rise of Digitally-Native Brands

We first dived into Amazon and then dived into the technologies that try to replicate the Amazon experience. Now, I'll dive into the other perspective: removing the reliance on Amazon and apps and entering the direct-to-consumer space (D2C).

From a business fundamentals level, direct-to-consumer (D2C) brands are inherently digitally native and, therefore, attract digital-savvy customers. Looking at the circle visualization above, digitally-native vertical brands (DNVBs) position themselves in the midst of a legacy brand customer base, segments that were often overlooked yet show massive value due to the customer lifetime value potential.

A good example of this is Bonobos, the men's apparel brand that carved out a solid business by delivering 10x the value in men's apparel - better fit, custom style, easy fulfillment, and direct-to-consumer savings - to an underserved customer base that typically was ok with 1x value from legacy brands like Gap, Express or Banana Republic.

Talk about disruptive: Bonobos wowed and over-delivered for an underserved population that the big brands assumed were ok with the status quo.

Most of us know D2C as simply brands that cut out the middleman retailer (which makes sense from the previous reason we just discussed: remove the middleman). Instead of selling through retailers or Amazon, go straight to the customer and deliver better products, lower prices, and digitally-native experiences.

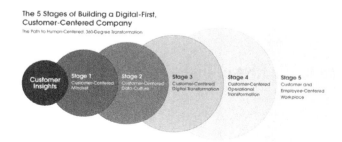

The 5 Stages of Building a Digital-First, Customer-Centered Company

According to Harvard Business Review, however, D2C goes deeper than just cutting out the middleman. D2C brands are the epitome of customer-first and data-driven, and that's what steers their business.

The competitive advantage of D2C is the following: 1) they have a deep knowledge of their customer base, and 2) they have control over their customer file. Overall, D2C brands know exactly who their customer is, what makes them buy, what drives their loyalty, what makes them churn, and what makes them passionate. The D2C mindset goes far beyond just cutting out the middleman.

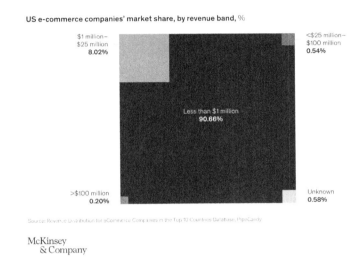

US e-commerce companies' market share, by revenue band, %

Source: Revenue Distribution for eCommerce Companies in the Top 10 Countries Database, PipeCandy

McKinsey
& Company

But most brands are not truly digitally native from the ground up. And because the majority of brands don't have a truly inherent D2C mindset from the ground up, as shown by the above visualization, they lose customers to the best D2C brands in their niche.

According to McKinsey, the top e-commerce brands - the $1M to $25M and $25M to $100M, which only make up less than 10% of the total e-commerce US landscape - are increasingly digitally native, which helped them scale. Makes sense: 86% of customers crave better shopping experiences, and digitally-native brands are positioned to deliver on that promise.

So, how should the smaller e-commerce brand compete with a digitally-native D2C brand? It's nearly impossible without a top-down philosophical change (see that HBR visualization again). That's why D2C brands are growing 3x faster than normal e-commerce brands like you. In fact, 90% of the brands in that graph struggle to break free from $1M+ a year simply due to a lack of being truly digitally native. In other words, most brands talk the D2C talk but aren't walking the walk.

Let's go a little bit deeper into that point. As mentioned before, Harvard Business Review says digital-first and customer-centric are really synonymous. And the reason for that is that they focus everything they do on the customer: from customer insights to customer data to customer-centric training for their entire staff.

Because D2C is customer-centric and digitally native, savvy customers gravitate to them... leaving you as part of the 90% remaining. This customer-centric philosophy is why the best of D2C - Brooklinen, Casper, Glossier, Warby Parker, and on - have grown into billion-dollar unicorns in a few short years.

D2C brands are better positioned than you are to attract the modern digital-savvy customer. They were born into a digital world, and they capture the online customers you once had.

To quote the movie *It's a Good Day to Die Hard* (I'm a big Bruce Willis fan!), most brands - 90% of them - are a Timex watch in a digital world, and that's why time is not on your side for keeping customers loyal.

D2C is positioned to capture your customers with their top-down digitally native mindset, and that's reason number six for why customers will leave you. But the news gets even worse with the next and final reason.

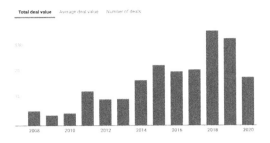

Total deal value    Average deal value    Number of deals

2008  2010  2012  2014  2016  2018  2020

# Reason 7. Direct-to-Consumer War Chests

The graph above shows the total venture capital (VC) funding for D2C brands over the past decade; as you can see, funding increased 45% annually, dipping slightly during a pandemic year due to, well, a pandemic as well as a more selective D2C investing attitude.

The war chests are open, and cash is flowing from Silicon Valley, banks, and Shark Tanks. So, what are all those D2C brands using that cash for?

I picture them swimming in all those dollars like Scrooge McDuck, knowing there's another VC down the road who will keep adding more to the war chest. Wishful thinking.

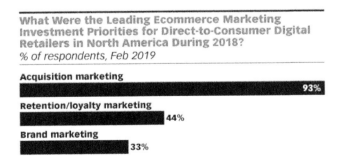

What Were the Leading Ecommerce Marketing Investment Priorities for Direct-to-Consumer Digital Retailers in North America During 2018?
% of respondents, Feb 2019

Acquisition marketing
93%

Retention/loyalty marketing
44%

Brand marketing
33%

According to eMarketer, we know where all that cash went: 93% of D2C brands prioritized one goal above all: acquisition. Their whole strategy is to get new customers. Let me rephrase that: their whole strategy is to get YOUR customers.

And because they're extremely well-funded by multiple VC sources and tasked with scaling their brand fast, D2C brands can afford to have better offers, faster fulfillment, and better experience in order to seduce customers away from your brand.

## D2C LANDSCAPE / LUMASCAPE 2018

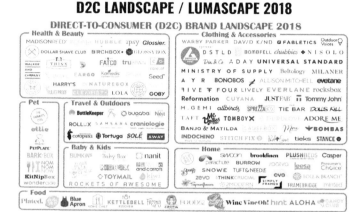

## D2C LANDSCAPE / LUMASCAPE 2021

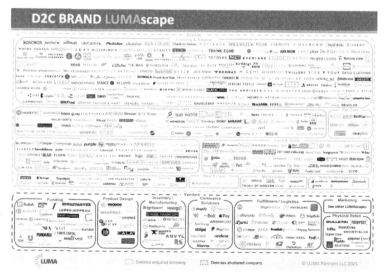

Look back a couple decades ago. Amazon scaled that model really well, right? Barnes & Noble and Border Books (who?) are a shell of their former selves because of Amazon's willingness to scale fast, forgo immediate profits, and invest in their flywheel. Modern-day D2C brands are doing the same exact thing. If the D2C war chest alone doesn't scare you, let's look at it from a different angle.

Your brand also needs to acquire customers, and generally, that requires ad spend. Yet, the more D2C brands spend on ads, the more competition for the ad space. More ad bidding means higher ad prices. Higher ad prices equal lower returns on YOUR ad spend.

Not only do you lose out on existing customers being seduced by D2C brands, but you also face higher acquisition costs that eat into your margins. Having a well-funded war chest is now doubly challenging for your brand when it comes to keeping customers or acquiring new ones.

I'm going to scare you more. Look at the LUMAscapes, a mind-blowing visualization of the state of D2C. The number of brands competing in your niche literally quadrupled. All that VC funding helped bring more players into your industry - case in point: in 2010, there were 25 mattress brands; in 2022, there are 170 brands - and all of them have one goal. Acquire your customers.

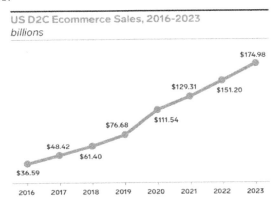

US D2C Ecommerce Sales, 2016-2023
*billions*

If you're reading this book, you may be a D2C brand, and you may benefit from a fantastic war chest. But can you compete with the new brand coming into your space, poaching your customers from you?

Remember that graph from Reason #6 - 90% of brands are only at $1M or less, so the chances that you have a war chest to match are slim to none. The marketing budgets between you and a well-funded D2C brand simply don't align.

They could spend $10M+ on paid search a year, where you struggle to justify $10K or $100K monthly. The playing field isn't leveled, budgets aren't aligned, you're outspent... and customers defect.

Go back to the McKinsey statistic: 76% of customers changed stores, brands, or shopping habits during COVID-19. Customer loyalty is at an all-time low, and when you're outspent with ads, offers and value, your customers can get easily seduced by rich D2C brands. And that's reason number seven why customers are leaving your brand.

## The Challenges & Solutions

The challenges from Amazon, Silicon Valley apps, and D2C are huge. Let's recap these top seven reasons:

1. **Amazon sets the pace; huge yet faceless marketplace**
2. **Amazon owns product search & personalization**
3. **Amazon built an unbeatable conglomerate of value**
4. **Amazon's perfected flywheel is three years ahead**
5. **Apps & Meta are middlemen between you and customers**
6. **D2C Brands are more digitally-native than you**
7. **D2C war chests aim to acquire your customers**

Picture that snowglobe again and ask yourself: am I in the best position to capture all those up-in-the-air customers, AND am I in the best position to stop customers from leaving my brand for the competition?

Based on these seven reasons, the top brands are better positioned than you to capture, retain and grow customer loyalty. They're well-funded, digitally native, have higher value offerings, and meet the customer where they expect to be met.

The barriers to success are getting higher and higher, and the e-commerce game is getting more and more difficult to play, let alone succeed.

Luckily, there is a solution where the small business can compete to win in a very crowded marketplace and with the deck stacked against them.

**If you can't win the game, then you have to change the game**. Let's look at those customer loyalty challenges again and focus on overcoming each hurdle individually.

- **If Amazon is a huge faceless marketplace, your brand can compete by "having a face"** and creating a unique story that binds you to the customer. As the data will show you, customers are demanding brands to put people over profits. Creating a story, mission, and reason for existing is how you'll win over the modern-day customer.
- **If Amazon owns product search and personalization, you refocus your efforts on excellent customer personalization.** Everyone has a pain point they need to solve with the product they bought; Amazon may solve the product challenge, but you can solve the product AND the pain point through customer experience, personalization and empathy.

- **If Amazon has built an unbeatable conglomerate of value, you build a community of value that is equally unbeatable.** You create a tribe of customers who are passionate about your mission, story, products, and services and will care about you because you care about them. Remember: no one cares about what you know until they know how much you care.

- **If Amazon has perfected the logistics and fulfillment channels, delivering products faster and on-demand, you create that perfect omni-channel experience**, delivering service, experiences, education, and expertise on demand. You have the tools to be omnipresent, just like the top brands. Use them!

- **If Silicon Valley apps and social media are becoming the middleman between you and the customer, you can change the game by owning the customer relationship entirely** from start to finish. From the first visit to post-purchase, acquisition to retention, you will own every step of the relationship and start weaning off profit-reducing middlemen to compete.

- **If D2C brands are more digitally native than you and gaining digitally-savvy customers, you need to become as customer-centric and data-driven as they are.** This solution is one of the hardest to fully internalize, yet the technology to jumpstart your customer-centric transition is fully available to you. Not only can you change the game, you can level the playing field very quickly at the same time.

- **If D2C brands have unlimited acquisition funds and are focused on acquiring your customers, focus your marketing funds on customer retention and keeping your customers.** You'll learn the Pareto Principle shortly - 80% of your revenue comes from just 20% of your customers - and discover that retaining and growing customers beats any acquisition strategy, hands-down.

If you can't win the game, then you have to change the game. Let's pair up the threats and opportunities clearly so you can visualize the challenges and start creating actionable strategies:

| Challenges: | Solutions: |
|---|---|
| ✗ Amazon is a Huge yet Faceless Marketplace | ☑ Create a Brand Face & Unique Story |
| ✗ Amazon Owns Search & Product Personalization | ☑ Focus on Customer Personalization |
| ✗ Amazon Perfects The Logistics & Fulfillment Channels | ☑ Create Perfect Omni-Channel Experience |
| ✗ Amazon's Building a Conglomerate of Value | ☑ Build a Community of Value |
| ✗ Apps & Meta = Middleman Between Customer & You | ☑ Own the Customer Relationship Entirely |
| ✗ D2C = Digitally-Native and Data-Driven | ☑ Be Customer-Centric & Data-Driven |
| ✗ D2C Have Unlimited Acquisition Funds | ☑ Focus on Retention Funds & Investments |

In short, these are the seven marketing solutions that will help you stave off the seven loyalty challenges you'll face this year and beyond. **Repeat this line again: if you can't win the game, then you have to change the game.** But even if you don't change the game, leveling the playing field is already a major win in the face of the huge, well-funded, omnipresent e-commerce competitors out there.

I can almost sense a "change the game" strategy starting to take form in your mind, and if you're anything like me, you're excited and ready to take on the world. But part of being a data-driven marketer, which any strong e-commerce brand needs at their disposal, means you need to establish two next steps:

1. **A solid plan for rolling these tactics out;** more specifically, which marketing channels will offer the best results possible
2. **Establishing key performance indicators (KPIs)** that determine if the strategy is working.

So, let's set up a litmus test to determine which tactics will help you stop hemorrhaging customers while also positioning you for future success in customer retention and growth.

# The Litmus Test

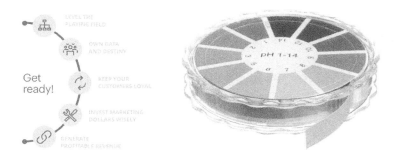

To truly measure the results of a great marketing strategy, let's go high level to start and then bring it down to eye level to implement. You could go super-granular and talk about the clicks, opens, likes, shares, tweets, comments, conversions, sessions, and on and on. But we're not there yet.

Let's think big picture to start and drill down from there. Some of the big performance indicators should be as follows:

1. **The strategy must help you level the playing field.** Any strategy you roll out should help you get to a place where you can, at the very least, compete. Namely, do we have the right technologies, staff, mindset, and website to compete from here on? If your brand mindset can simply level the playing field with Amazon's mindset or the D2C mindset, that's already a big win. If you can become more customer-centric instead of product-centric like the top brands, that's another step towards leveling the playing field. Overall, if the strategy you roll out helps level the playing field, you'll be in a better spot than 90% of e-commerce brands.

2. **The strategy must help you maintain ownership of data and destiny**. Relying on apps or technology to fill in your gaps is essential to e-commerce. But if you're relying too heavily on a certain technology, you've

sacrificed ownership of your destiny. As I said before, incorporating ShopRunner or DoorDash is good; relying on them to fuel your business is terrifying. Any strategy you roll out must focus on primarily owning your data and owning your future at all costs.

3. **The strategy must result in customer loyalty to your brand.** There are a lot of apps, methods, and tactics for increasing customer loyalty. A quick Google search will yield hundreds of loyalty apps to use. The smartest way, though, will be the method that allows you to direct the loyalty to you as a business, not just to your technology or medium. Any strategy you roll out must connect customers to your brand and create true loyalty.

4. **The strategy must invest your dollars smarter**. Trying to brute-force your way into relevance with a blitz of cash and tons of ad spend is nearly impossible. Budgets are tight, margins are tight, and return on ad spend could be slim; spending copious amounts of cash has a lot of challenges. Consistency plays a role as well; certain months, you can swing the cash investment, other months, you can't, and the inconsistency is a killer. The right strategy means your limited dollars will work smarter for you and won't equate to outspending your competition (because you never will be able to!)

5. **The strategy must generate profits, not just revenue.** You're in business to make a profit. It's not enough to roll out a strategy that drives unprofitable revenue or simply breaks even on your investment. You have to make a profit, take money home, feed your family, pay your bills, staff up and invest in the future. Bringing in $1.50 for $1 spent may not cut it. On top of that, you need to generate revenue that's profitable, predictable, and sustainable so you can pay salaries, rents, and IT costs as well as your own take-home pay! The strategy must generate profits, not just revenue.

If you can find that one consistent strategy that will check off all these boxes, you will truly be competing to win. Missing one single KPI on this litmus test may be ok in the short term but won't be survivable in the long term.

For example, you may level the playing field, but if it's at the expense of spending billions in cash, you're literally banking everything and not saving for a rainy day (like a pandemic!)

Another example: if you solve keeping customers loyal, but you make no profits, you don't have a really great future and zero runway for other business investments.

Hitting some of these KPIs is great. Hitting all of them should be the ultimate goal. Now, let's dive into the four most popular strategies that brands implement to try and win customer loyalty.

## Option 1: Invest in Social Media

Let's dive into one of the more popular options that brands are using to grow customer loyalty: organic and paid social media.

Everyone's on social media. You can run ads, leverage Instagram influencers, and build organic reach with gorgeous videos and posts. The social platforms are endless as well - Twitter, Pinterest, TikTok, and others are joining Meta as platforms with great consumer reach. You can run funnel-based ads and retargeting ads, track user behavior on your website and build lookalike audiences as well. Investing in a competitive strategy on social media sounds very appealing.

So, let's see if social media, as a whole, helps you compete with the top seven reasons customers leave.

✓ **Yes, you can create a unique brand story with social media.** It works. Brands are out there running great ads, telling great stories through video and carousels, and leveraging user-generated content in their content.

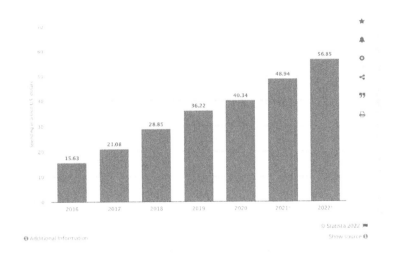

In fact, look at the steady increase in social media ad spend. Social ad spend is consistently growing at around 50% every year. And even if you settle for a low return on ad spend (ROAS), it's not a bad investment.

**Facebook Page Organic Reach**

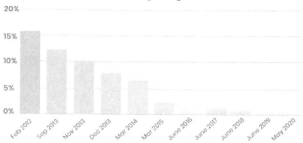

Here's the downside, though. With all that paid social traffic and investment, organic reach is taking a major hit. Across all major platforms, social posts are simply not reaching people all the time.

And the traffic that does show up to your website? They increasingly seem to be automated bots that inflate your traffic numbers. In order to maximize the potential of social media, you have to actually spend money to tell your story; organically, you won't find much of an audience.

Long story short: yes, check that box. You can create a brand face and unique story using social media; you simply have to pay to play.

✖ **Here's where social media doesn't work: it does not do great customer personalization.** You can build lookalike audiences and do some fantastic segmentation options - though still limited primarily to Facebook engagement only - but when it comes to personalizing the ads to every user, you become very limited.

Retargeting ads with items customers shopped or looked at is possible, but that's a minor transactional part of personalization. You're not able to get to the root of this customer's challenges, needs, and pain points using social media. Segmentation may be pretty vast, but personalization is quite lacking on social media.

As of the writing of this book, a recent Wall Street Journal article highlighted that Meta stumbled trying to navigate their paid e-commerce ad options. So, personalization via social media does not check that box.

✓ **Social media is becoming better at crafting a perfect omnichannel experience.** More and more customers are DM'ing brands on Messenger, Instagram, and WhatsApp.

Brands are using social as customer service, encouraging reviews, dialogue, and education. So, yes, we can give social media an omni-channel check because it's being used the way it should be used: being social.

✓ **You could also build a community of value out there, although you're kind of leasing space on Meta and not really owning it.** The upside of social is that you can build a tribe and share positive news, great products, and create active groups.

The downside is that one black eye will go viral really fast. Take Peloton; as I'm writing this, they've faced major stumbles in their business - TV deaths, product recalls, and slowdowns in demand - and the news spread like wildfire across social media. But if your brand and product are high quality, you can build a strong community of value with the right people. So, let's give the benefit of the doubt and check this box.

✗ **But you're still placing social media at the center of everything you're doing.** You're still relying on Meta to be the middleman for your story, success, and tribe. That's a major red eye and fails this checkpoint. Doesn't need much more explanation here; you can't say you own the customer relationship when Meta is in the middle of it all.

✗ **Because Meta wants to remain the middleman, they have little incentive to share data with you.** In their drive to remain the middleman, Meta, Twitter, and even Google will not give you enough data-driven insights to help you make bigger business decisions.

The data they do provide is geared around helping you run better ads, build better audiences, establish in-social groups and increase social engagement. Those insights don't help much if you're trying to run an e-commerce store beyond social media.

✖ **The biggest fail of rolling out a social media strategy to help you compete is that everyone else can do the same thing.** Amazon, D2C startups, and unicorn brands are doing the exact same thing right now; they're already three years ahead. In fact, the top 1% actually get more help from Meta than you do, simply because they spend more. So, you definitely won't overcome their budgets, reach and influence using social media. You're outspent, outreached, and outgunned.

Let's recap. Going all-in on a social media strategy to help you compete against the top brands has pros and cons:

✓ Social helps you create a brand face, story and mission
✖ Social is highly limited in customer personalization
✓ Social establishes a great omni-channel experience
✓ Social helps build a community of value that's unbreakable
✖ You lose full ownership over the customer relationship
✖ Social has scarce data to help you be customer-centric
✖ Brands can do the same on social & outspend you

Investing in social media, organic and paid, does not hit every single checkbox, and you still remain highly vulnerable. Although you may be fine with rolling this strategy out regardless of its failings, remember that a leaky bucket will eventually lose all water. It just takes longer.

As a second check, let's run the social media option through our litmus test to see exactly if maybe it passes all those tests.

1. **Social does not help you level the playing field.** The top brands can do the exact same thing you're doing.
2. **You lose ownership of data and destiny.** You're relying on Facebook and Meta to do that.
3. **You are investing your dollars smarter.** If you have a great paid social team and a generous budget, you can see ROI here. The downside is attribution to social media efforts is kind of low. And then there's Apple with their iOS updates screwing up your results. But social is a better investment than other channels.

4. **It doesn't keep customers loyal.** If you're spending money to keep your customers, you have bigger problems. Paid social is best for customer acquisition, not retention, and your brand, service, experience, and product should retain customers.

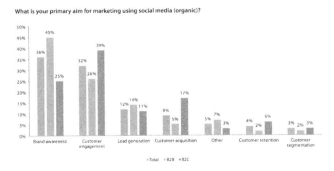

5. **It can generate profitable revenue.** Some brands could see as much as 20x returns on paid social, so, again, if you have a crackerjack team on paid social, you can be profitable. Until the next Apple iOS or Meta algorithm change, that is!

So, the litmus test fails with only 2 out of 5 KPIs that actually help your business stave off competition and keep customers loyal.

✘ Level the playing field.
✘ Maintain ownership of data & destiny
✓ Invest your dollars smarter
✘ Keep customers loyal
✓ Generate profitable revenue

Once again, this isn't a knock on the power of social media. You should definitely have a social media strategy in place regardless of this analysis. This recap is simply showing that there may be a better (or worse) strategy out there that will help your brand keep its customers and stave off the competition.

## Option 2: Invest in Paid Search

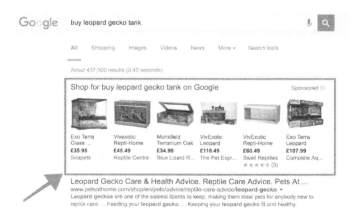

Let's dive into option two. Maybe it's time to focus on Google search, Google Shopping ads, or Google My Business (GMB). Sounds like a great idea.

A Google strategy is mandatory for every e-commerce store. Tons of e-commerce brands run ads, they're attracting shoppers in hunt mode, and they convert really well. If you have a great content plan and a well-designed website, you'll experience fantastic organic reach in search, yielding profitable sales.

On top of that, GMB helps local stores compete in search through maps, reviews, and store hours. So, let's go line item by line item to determine if a customer loyalty strategy should be heavily reliant on paid or organic search.

✓ **Google has great scale, especially for brick and mortar.** You can do a lot, including keywords, questions, phrases, videos, and more. Search "find leopard gecko tanks near me," discover reviews, and even find pictures of products in use.

Gmail and YouTube are ubiquitous in users' lives, and Google certainly has great scale and reach.

✗ **Google is getting dinged on product search, though.** Remember, Amazon owns 78% of product search, so Google's left with the remainder. In addition, depending on your industry,

Amazon may be outbidding you on paid search and outmaneuvering you on organic search. Hard to check that box (especially if you have a limited budget).

✓ **Between Gmail, YouTube, Google Workspace, Google Forms, Google Drive and more, Google has some great omni-channel experiences.** Amp for Gmail can create dynamic emails for customer service and surveys. Google Docs is replacing Microsoft Word in everyday use at home, work, and school. And, well, who doesn't use Gmail? Google definitely plays a role in helping you go omni-channel.

DON'T START YOUTUBE BEFORE WATCHING THIS... 11K views · 2 days ago

AVOIDING CREATIVE BURNOUT 5.2K views · 1 week ago CC

MY BIGGEST BUSINESS MISTAKES 8.3K views · 2 weeks ago CC

THE YOUTUBE SALES MACHINE (DAY IN THE LIFE) 6.6K views · 3 weeks ago CC

✓ **Google and Youtube does help you create value adds and solve pain points,** especially if you're using every tool in Google's arsenal. As mentioned above, you can power customer surveys and in-email dialogues. You can create Podcasts, start Hangout chats, build community groups, and more. Google Analytics alone is table stakes for e-commerce reporting and analytics. And let's not forget all the value from YouTube, which is owned by Google. DIY videos, custom playlists, and live broadcasts all help create a nice amount of added YouTube value for your brand. That could definitely hit that checkbox.

✗ **Google is still the middleman.** Essentially, you're banking everything you're doing on Google, and you have to pay for that investment. Trading in one middleman, like Meta, for another isn't going to help long term. One of the biggest challenges for Google and Meta: customer privacy. If legislation hits and affects their business model, you run the risk of being dragged down with big tech.

✖ **Like Meta, Google has little incentive to share the immense amounts of data that they receive from search, videos, and Gmail.** Google parses out limited amounts of data to help you run a better business - Google Analytics, to name one - but overall, truly predictive customer data isn't exportable and usually reserved for those spending money on ads. So, you're not being very customer-centric or data-driven by banking your competitive strategy on Google's limited data.

✖ **Once again, Google is available to everyone.** Brands can outspend you on ads, run better videos, and engage in better SEO tactics, and they will. The playing field isn't very leveled if you can be outspent.

Let's recap. Going all-in on a paid search strategy fails four out of seven checkpoints; customers can still be lost in these gaps.

✓  Paid search has scale, especially for brick & mortar
✖ Paid search is losing the product search capabilities
✓  Paid search creates an entry-level multi-channel experience
✓  Paid search & Google value-stacks their suite of tools
✖ Google remains the middleman between you and customers
✖ Google shares limited actionable customer data
✖ Brands can outspend you on Google and other search engines

Maybe paid search passes that litmus test, though, right? Maybe a stronger Google investment is a good enough strategy to roll out and see how it goes. Let's check:

1. **Google does not help you level the playing field.** The top brands are doing the same thing you're doing. And it's like major league vs. single-A ball.
2. **You lose ownership of data and destiny**. If everyone relies on Google Analytics, you simply don't have the power to make your own decisions. You're pretty much

looking backward at what occurred rather than looking forward to predict business outcomes. From a customer point of view, Google's certainly not going to give you enough data to fuel your decisions, except if you're running ads on their platform.

3. **You are investing your dollars smarter.** Same as social media, if you have a great paid search team and a generous budget, you can see ROI here. But bear in mind - see the graph below - Amazon is outbidding you as the largest advertiser in the world, so either you lose the ad spot or pay a lot more.

## Amazon Tops
## U.S. Advertiser Ranking

Leading advertisers in the United States, based on total U.S. ad spending in 2019

| Advertiser | Ad Spending |
|---|---|
| amazon | $6.88b |
| COMCAST | $6.14b |
| AT&T | $5.48b |
| P&G | $4.28b |
| Walt Disney | $3.15b |
| Alphabet | $3.13b |
| verizon | $3.07b |
| Charter | $3.04b |

4. **Google doesn't keep customers loyal.** They're primarily an acquisition channel, not retention. The job of Google is to bring you customers, not keep them. In addition, last I checked, your website's search engine is either 1) powered by Google or 2) pales in comparison to Google, so your best customers are using Google to search for products more than using your site search.

5. **Google can help you make a profit.** You can definitely be profitable by using Google ads. After piecing together the offer, free shopping, free returns, and advertising, you may not net much, but the potential for profit is

certainly there. Until an algorithm change or bidding increase forces your prices up!

So, investing further into a Google strategy doesn't hit every checkbox nor pass our litmus test.

✗ Level the playing field.
✗ Maintain ownership of data & destiny
✓ Invest your dollars smarter
✗ Keep customers loyal
✓ Generate profitable revenue

## Option 3: Become an Amazon Merchant

This option is more controversial. If you can't beat Amazon, join Amazon, right? If acquiring customers is a priority for you, this could be a great option; Amazon's flywheel does provide a lot of traffic for you to capitalize on.

Let's take a look at this option for keeping customers loyal.

✓ **Well, you certainly get traffic and benefit from Amazon's scale.** A good win there. You may have some challenges from competitors on the same website, but you definitely get eyeballs to tell your story.

✓ **You'd benefit from Amazon's search.** The search traffic coming in is great for your business, and you could sell a lot!

✗ **You definitely have no omni-channel experience because everything is on Amazon.** The whole customer experience - even shipping the product (FBA) - is all owned by Amazon. Truly a faceless e-commerce experience, and you lose an opportunity to build a brand.

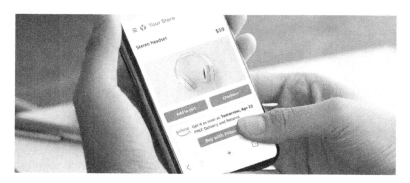

✗ **You can take advantage of being a Prime customer, yet it may mean lower margins for you.** If you can swing it, great, but generally, lower margins aren't sustainable. And customers are expecting goods and services faster, so if you're NOT a Prime seller, you lose out to the competitor who is. In addition, Amazon's 'Buy Now with Prime' option on your website may be good for shoppers but not necessarily for your business (see the next reason). Overall, if you can't make a healthy profit, you can't stay in business.

✗ **Amazon becomes the middleman.** You rely on Amazon for everything you sell, ship, and restock. If Amazon likes you, you can sell on their marketplace. If you commit a single infraction, your business gets shut down. And if Amazon really loves you, they could copy your product and private label it under one of their hundreds of private label brands, like Amazon Basics. The Wall Street Journal called this out in the article below; Amazon scooped up data from its own sellers to launch competing products. Amazon ensures loyalty remains with them, the middleman, and not the brand.

✘ **There's zero customer data to export to you, so you can't be customer-centric nor data-driven** even if you wanted to. Not only do you not need it - since you've joined Amazon and primarily selling there, obviously! - Amazon has no incentive to help you sell directly to customers. These are Amazon's customers, their market, their data, and their decisions.

✘ **Finally, there's no customer retention option**. You barely have any way to communicate with your customers, in fact: masked email addresses, limited phone numbers, and a very transactional relationship. You're fully focused on acquisition ads, and, well, other brands can do the same. Remember, there's a reason why Nike delisted.

Joining Amazon is certainly the worst of the three options if you want to compete and keep customers loyal; the strategy fails on five out of seven checkboxes. If you're trying to create a successful, profitable, and customer-intimate business that beats the competition, teaming up with Amazon ensures that never happens.

✓ Amazon's scale guarantees sales and some story-telling
✓ Good opportunities for product personalization due to search
✘ Zero omni-channel experience, just Amazon experience
✘ You benefit from the value but lack community building
✘ Amazon is the middleman for the entire time

✘ You own very little customer data

✘ There's no retention option, only acquisition ad spending.

Maybe it passes the litmus test.

1. **Amazon does help level the playing field.** Correction, you give up the playing field and concede the game to Amazon. But here's an interesting statistic: brands on Amazon say that their biggest competitor is actually Amazon! Ironic; if you think the playing field was leveled, you just traded one competitor for another! Plus, you're still competing against the same brands on Amazon as you were off Amazon. But for the sake of argument, we'll say joining Amazon helps "level the playing field" in a bizarre way.

**Brands' Biggest Source of Competition**

Brands on Amazon      All Brands

- National or Global Brands
- Direct-to-Consumer Brands
- Amazon's Private Label Brands
- Private Label Brands
- Emerging Brands

2. **You lose ownership of data and destiny.** Guess what? It's not your data anymore. It's Amazon's. Read your fine print; Amazon determines your destiny.

3. **You're not investing your dollars smarter.** You kind of just gave up, so any investments are Amazon-based.

Traffic, search, and purchases are all dependent on Amazon's algorithm. Even Amazon Advertising may not work as well with so much competition for space.

4. **Amazon doesn't keep your customers loyal.** They're loyal to Amazon. End sentence. Period. Stamp it.

5. **Amazon won't help you make a profit.** Interestingly enough, 57% of brands still need and rely on their own website for sales. They can't just rely on Amazon to make their numbers. If you're a one-person operation, maybe you could swing to a profit, but brands like the ones reading this book may have a tough go at it.

> 66 57% of brands still need and rely on their own website for sales, and 42% of survey respondents currently sell products at their own brick-and-mortar stores.

Joining Amazon fails the litmus test. You've given up any chance of keeping customers loyal to your brand, mission, and products:

✓ Level the playing field
✗ Maintain ownership of data & destiny
✗ Invest your dollars smarter
✗ Keep customers loyal
✗ Generate profitable revenue

Three potential marketing strategies are down, and you're not much closer to developing a plan to keep customers loyal. A social media strategy and a search strategy offer some areas of improvement yet not enough to truly remain competitive in the long run. Going the Amazon route indicates that you've truly given up and prefer to join the competition rather than go solo.

Now, let's dive into the final strategy that the top e-commerce brands focus on to keep customers loyal in the face of steep competition.

## Option 4: Invest in Email & SMS

Let's dive into option number four: investing in customer-centric channels like email, SMS and CRM. The fact that the industry refers to email & SMS as the most customer-centric channel already shows promise. CRM itself stands for customer relationship marketing, so obviously, that strategy is all about the customer. And email is a constant in people's lives; most people have two emails - one for home and one for work. So, let's dive into solution number four in more depth.

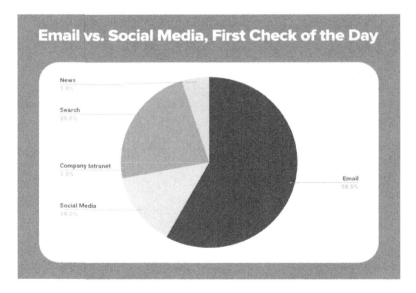

✓ **You can create a brand personality, story, and mission using email & SMS quite easily**. From welcome workflows to nurture programs, it's quite easy and inexpensive to tell your story over a series of emails and texts.

✓ As mentioned above, **email & SMS excel in customer personalization** simply because it's the most personalized way of communication. Email is the first check of the day for most people; we check our email right away when we wake up and right before we go to sleep. Yes, people do the same with social media, but there are two emails to check - work and personal. Double the opportunity for customer personalization.

Number of e-mail users worldwide from 2017 to 2025
*(in millions)*

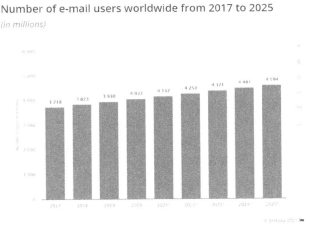

✓ **Email & SMS combined creates a seamless omni-channel experience**. Think about it - make a purchase, trigger a confirmation email, send a shipping notification text, send a thank you email, and sign in to your account with an email.

An email and phone number is the one data point that personalizes every stage of the customer journey. Go deeper: you can send that email and phone number to Google and Facebook and personalize the ad experiences for every customer as well. That's true personalization.

✓ **By simply joining a brand's email list means you're entering a community of like-minded people**. You don't even need to make a purchase, yet you already unlock community value from content, expertise, promotions, and selection. Every email can facilitate additional community building within Facebook group membership, YouTube subscribers, or Instagram followers. And where do all your data points reside? They reside within your ESP or CRM, creating a truly 360-degree view of every customer in the community.

✓ **Email & SMS helps you own the customer relationship entirely.** Once you own the email or phone number, you own that one data point that is unique to every single person. It's the definition of customer-centric.

As mentioned above, you can use that single customer-centric data point to power every other channel out there. Need a Facebook lookalike audience of your best customers? Send an email list to Facebook. Need a product loyalist list to kickstart your ads on Google? Send phone numbers to Google. Want to pair online and offline data for every customer? An email or phone number stitches it all together.

✓ **Email & SMS is all about retention.** When other brands spend heavily on acquiring, you spend more on retaining. It costs 600% more to acquire a customer than it does to retain a customer, so you're already going to be ahead budget-wise. You may get a one-time customer from Google or Facebook, and email, SMS and CRM will focus on growing that one-time buyer into a lifetime buyer.

**Investing in a customer-centric, data-driven email, SMS and CRM strategy passes every single checkbox** on how you can compete with the top brands and ensure customer loyalty.

✓ **Email & SMS creates a brand face & unique story**
✓ **Email & SMS excels in customer personalization**
✓ **Email & SMS creates perfect omni-channel experiences**
✓ **Email & SMS builds communities of value**
✓ **Email & SMS lets you own the customer relationship**

✓ **Email & SMS is the one main customer-centric channel**
✓ **Email & SMS is focused primarily on retention & loyalty**

Let's go deeper into what makes email & SMS the best option for keeping e-commerce customers loyal in a very fickle marketplace.

## Solution 1. Email & SMS = Your Story, Your Terms

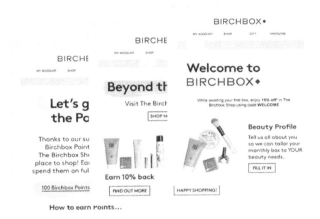

**Email, SMS and CRM allows you to tell your story** on your terms because it has more real estate for story-telling. You have the potential to create a welcome series, a nurture series, re-engagement series, and more, all dedicated to building your brand and creating a relationship.

In addition, subscribers elect to opt in and hear from you, inviting you to share why your brand is unique. Going deeper, you can personalize the story to every customer using recommendations, send time optimization, and dynamic content elements, such as store hours for local audiences. These make your story feel more personalized to every user.

Email is a free channel with no ad spend, so you don't have to worry about sacrificing margins just to share what you're about.

In fact, email converts at a higher level, and customers will pay a premium or full price if they love your story. No discount needed!

And finally, email & SMS can be automated 24/7 and continuously run with multi-touches for every part of your story.

With more story-telling real estate, personalization elements, and 24/7 capabilities, you can truly become an e-commerce store with a face, story, and mission, beating the faceless Amazon experience hands down.

## Solution 2. Email & SMS = Personalization at Scale.

Solution number two: you prioritize customer personalization over product personalization. Here's why email, SMS and CRM are at the top of that list.

While personalization is a top priority, only 15% of retailers have fully implemented personalization across all channels.

Remember, 84% of customers demand personalization, and although personalization is a top priority for brands, only 15% of retailers have fully implemented it across all channels.

The way to achieve great personalization is to connect with the person behind the email. You can't go connect on a one-to-one level with Facebook profiles using a Facebook ad. You can only do that with email & SMS and dive deep into personalization based on their buying history, behaviors, preferences, and actions.

Using email & SMS, you can personalize every level of communication - for free, mind you! - with relevant content, categories, or products.

The more personalized the communication, the more impact; the more impact, the fewer emails need to be sent to elicit a response. Imagine that: better communications, fewer emails, and more revenue. Customer personalization is truly at the center of a great customer experience.

But personalization via email & SMS can even go beyond retention; it has applications for acquisition as well. By knowing your customer affinities, purchase history, preferences, and browsing habits, you can bucket people into segmented cohorts. A great example of this are VIP customers who pay full price. You can then send their emails or phone numbers to Facebook and Google and find more VIP customers just like them using Facebook's Lookalike Audiences and Google's Similar Audiences.

You can't export Facebook data on your VIP customers and send it over to your CRM; there's no way to do it, and any Facebook data is useless once it's pulled out of Facebook. Email & SMS is the only way to truly 1) create 1:1 personalization for every customer and 2) scale that personalization across all your channels, so you become omnipresent.

## Solution 3. Email & SMS = Omni-channel and Omnipresent

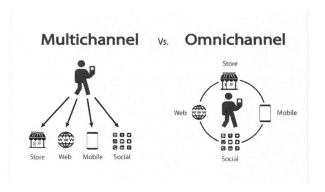

Let's talk about solution number three: email and SMS help stitch the customer experience together, both online and offline. That's a near-perfect omni-channel experience.

See the visual above. In the past decade, most brands were focused on being multi-channel, creating good experiences for each customer, wherever they shop. Problems arose when customers expected brands to know their history, preferences, and loyalty everywhere they shop; if a ten-time online shopper opted to visit a local store, brands seldomly treated them like the VIPs they were. Email & SMS changed all that.

Currently, the top brands have adapted and pivoted everything around the customer, not the channel. And the only way to revolve around the customer is to have a single unique identifier to literally pinpoint them. That identifier is an email or phone number. Email & SMS is the only way to stitch your phone, store, and online data together.

**Why personalization must be a top priority:**

**10–15%**
uplift potential in
revenue and retention

**10–30%**
more efficient marketing
and cost savings

**3–5%**
increased customer
acquisition

**5–10%**
higher satisfaction
and engagement

**... yet only 15% of marketers say they have fully implemented personalized marketing**

Want proof? Think about when you go into Walgreens and scan your loyalty card or Kroger when you shop for groceries, or even Starbucks when you use their app. Walgreens asks you to punch in your phone number for rewards; why do they do that? So they can stitch your in-store purchases with your online purchases and personalize everything for you in perpetuity. All their marketing revolves around the email address or phone number you type in at checkout.

Think of the flip side: Walgreens doesn't ask you for your Facebook login, do they? I bet you can't even remember your password if they did ask! Starbucks doesn't ask for your Instagram or Twitter handle. Brands can't create omni-channel personalization with social media but can with email & SMS.

Email & SMS unifies the customer data. By capturing an email or phone number, brands can now revolve everything around the customer, which, in turn, creates a better omni-channel experience.

# Solution 4. Email & SMS = Great Community Building

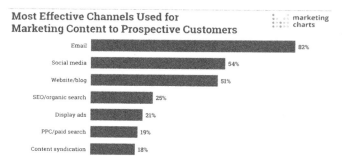

Most Effective Channels Used for Marketing Content to Prospective Customers

marketing charts

On to solution number four: email and SMS helps you build a community of value, beating a conglomerate of value. Remember, if you can't build a huge conglomerate value, you can build a huge community of value; email and SMS helps you do exactly that.

According to the statistic above, 82% of marketers say email is the most effective for marketing content. Similar to solution #1 about story-telling, you can build journeys, automations, nurture programs, and workflows all around your content.

Consumer expectations around societal contributions of businesses have risen ...

| 33% | 71% | 57% | 62% |
|---|---|---|---|
| stopped using a brand based on its social actions | will lose trust in a brand forever if it places profit over people | believe companies need to redefine their purpose to fight the pandemic | believe business is putting profits before people |

Being helpful and educational never takes a holiday. In the current business climate, however, creating a community requires a bit more from your brand. It requires a societal "people over profits" mindset.

Check out another McKinsey study: 33% of consumers stop using a brand because of its social actions, and 71% will lose trust in a brand forever if it places profit over people. In fact,

62% of respondents actually do believe businesses are currently putting profits before people.

Creating a community of value goes beyond content, customer service, Amazon Prime, and two-day shipping. Ironically, perhaps due to Amazon's faceless e-commerce experience, customers are demanding brands humanize their marketing with empathy, societal contributions, and mission-based values.

How can you best share your story, values, mission, and ethics? By building a tribe of like-minded people. The easiest and most impactful way to do that is with an email & SMS list where people want to hear from brands they share values with.

Email & SMS is also the cheapest way to build that tribe. No doubt, you can tell a story in a Facebook ad or video. But spending thousands of dollars daily on a video or carousel ad with very limited scroll-stopping attention span is not as efficient or impactful as free, consistent email & SMS story-telling over a 30-day period.

Look at the flow of a basic brand welcome series. In just a few days, brands can welcome people, tell their stories, bond by being helpful, incorporate social proof and offer help, all within an email welcome series. Every mode of communication - video, social, GIF, chat, text, phone - can all be part of an email & SMS workflow. Can you truly do that cost-effectively on search and social? No chance.

Using email & SMS to combine customer personalization, brand story-telling, and value-based marketing is the best way to build a community that's unbreakable.

## Solution 5. Email & SMS = 100% Customer-Centric.

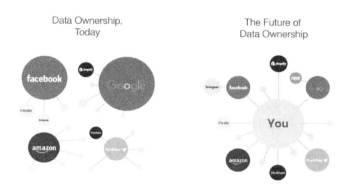

Looking at solution number five, you can easily see that email & SMS is a slam dunk when it comes to owning the customer relationship.

Looking at the current-state and future-state visualization above, data used to be siloed amongst different platforms. Google had some data, Facebook had some, your CRM had some, your store had some, and on and on. Having different puzzle pieces on different platforms didn't help brands create a unified customer view that could meaningfully move a business forward.

Which is why the future is all about complete data ownership by the brand. In order to create great customer personalization and stronger communities, you need to own the one customer-centric data point that customers revolve their world around: an email or phone number. When you own that one single identifier, you own the customer, and you can push that data out wherever you want. Instead of Google and Facebook owning part of your data, you own it all, and you can share that data with whomever and whenever you'd like.

Remember, this solution combats your reliance on Big Tech, apps, and Meta to power your business. Email & SMS removes those siloed data warehouses and unifies them under your ownership.

## Solution 6. Email & SMS = Better Customer Relationships.

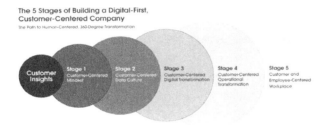

The 5 Stages of Building a Digital-First, Customer-Centered Company
The Path to Human-Centered, 360-Degree Transformation

As you're starting to see, email & SMS is combating every single challenge from the big brands, and the channel alone solves numerous pain points that go beyond customer loyalty.

And that's why solution number six - email & SMS levels the playing field by making your brand customer-centric - is more of a fundamental business shift than a solution.

If you revolve everything you do around the customer - your store, your website, your mobile experience, your app experience, your social media platform, and customer service - you become truly customer-centric. Revolving around the customer requires an email & SMS approach because, as mentioned above, it's the unique identifier of a customer.

In addition, as you saw from the Harvard Business Review workflow above, email & SMS helps you shift your e-commerce mindset from transactional to personal.

Instead of focusing solely on transactional relationships - did you order today, did you leave your cart, can I deliver this faster, etc. - your brand can focus on being personal and helpful - how can we help, can I help you achieve more, can I educate you, let's achieve goals, etc.

Being customer-first will trickle down to all levels of your business, and customers will love you for that. One of the biggest customer service challenges in e-commerce is mismatched expectations, and the biggest contributor to that issue is the lack of unified data. We'll get into that a bit more during the Post-Purchase Hourglass I talk about later on.

The evolution of your business to becoming truly customer-centric starts with customer insights. At the root of customer insights is email & SMS.

## Solution 7. Email & SMS = Higher Lifetime Value

The final solution - email & SMS focuses all your dollars on retention over acquisition, ensuring strong customer loyalty - is the cherry on top.

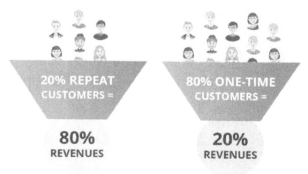

Few brands prioritize the Pareto Principle in their marketing primarily because it can be difficult to track in a world focused on instant gratification.

Imagine telling your boss or employees that in lieu of tracking revenue goals weekly, you'd rather track customer migrations from 1x buyers to 2x buyers; that's a KPI shift that, although super important, is hard to justify. Having said that, a data-driven, customer-centric e-commerce brand would welcome this approach... while also ensuring you hit your goals!

Applied to e-commerce, the Pareto Principle is straightforward and rewarding: 80% of your revenue comes from just 20% of your customers. So, if you spend more time nurturing customers into that 20% as well as preventing that 20% from leaving, you will automatically stave off customer churn. I think by now, you know that email & SMS is the only way to do this at scale, profitably and predictably.

You can't overestimate the importance of customer retention. Loyal customers are likely to buy more often from you and spend more money on each purchase. In fact, as shown below, studies by Bain & Company, along with Earl Sasser of the Harvard Business School, have shown that even a 5 percent increase in customer retention can lead to an increase in profits of between 25 and 95 percent.

Here's the beauty of retention: you have a home-court advantage. Those high-value 20% customers are already on your list and buying from you, so you simply have one job: show them you care, treat them well and keep them buying. Lose their trust, you lose them as a customer... and it's very expensive to try and replace a VIP customer.

The Pareto Principle goes a step further. 20% of your efforts will yield 80% of your rewards. As you focus all your investments on retention, you'll unlock the potential of marketing automations.

## 5% INCREASE IN RETENTION, 95% INCREASE IN PROFIT

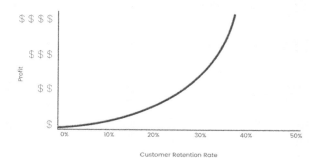

With a great strategy and team in place, you'll be able to create massive automations that will power 80% of your entire email revenue with minimal effort.

There may be lots of strategizing, designing, testing, and iterating at the start, but you'll eventually step away and let your email program run on autopilot... all due to the wisdom of the Pareto Principle.

Take it one step further. According to Bluecore, 74% of your customers right now are one-time buyers, and you've most likely acquired them at a loss or broke even.

Put together the ad costs, offer, shipping, and other elements, and those one-time buyers mean very little to your bottom line. On average, it costs 600% more to acquire a customer than retain one, so you spent a lot on one-time customers.

Worse, they'll never buy again without a similar incentive. Post-pandemic, millions of brands were inundated with one-time buyers and are struggling to convert them into loyalists. Your focus should be on converting, retaining, and growing the 20%, the VIPs, the best customers. It's a better use of your dollars and time. Existing customers convert better; they trust more, they have more data for personalization, and you have a relationship in place.

Instead of struggling to gain a $100 customer and trying to compete with the unlimited D2C war chest, focus on growing $100 customers into $1,000 customers... and then keeping them loyal long term. This retention strategy is only achievable using email, SMS and CRM, and that's solution number seven.

## Does it Pass the Litmus Test?

Like David against Goliath, email, SMS and CRM is the best way to keep customers loyal in the face of Amazon, Meta, Big Tech, and digitally-native D2C brands. The customer-centric, relationship-building efforts of email and SMS create unbreakable bonds, build brand affinity, connect people to your story and improve your marketing costs significantly.

But will an email, SMS and CRM strategy pass the Litmus Test we put in place? Does it check off boxes to ensure your business can scale profitably on its own momentum? Let's check this out:

1.  **Email & SMS changes the game... and playing field.** The top brands are focused on acquisition. They're using all those funds to acquire new customers, as shown by the graph previously. You're going to focus your investments on retention and build a foundation of customer loyalty. Once you level that playing field, you've changed the game on the big brands and can now confidently invest in an effective acquisition plan. Solve that, and you've created a marketing flywheel that changes the game.

2.  **You own the customer data and control your destiny.** Remember, if you own the primary customer data point - an email or phone number - you have control over the experience, messaging, and omni-channel approach. You're not relying on apps, Meta, or tech to "lend" you data on your customers.

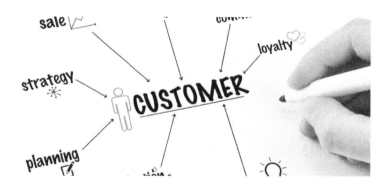

3.  **You're investing your dollars smarter.** Every dollar you spend on growing customer lifetime value directly leads to more profits. Recall that Bain and Company study showing that increasing customer retention rates

by 5% increases profits by 25% to 95%. With ROI like that, there's simply no better business investment.

4. **The relationship and community keep customers loyal.** Investing in the customer positions you for a long-term relationship. Email and SMS helps you think beyond the one-time purchase and excel in customer service, education, personalization, and experience. Even better, the community itself will keep every customer feeling like part of a family, rewarding your brand with enhanced customer loyalty.

5. **Email, SMS & CRM is the most profitable channel.** Email and SMS yields an average ROI of 3,800%, dwarfing every other marketing channel out there. So, you're definitely investing your dollars smarter and becoming more profitable.

Email and SMS pass every single checkbox on our Litmus Test. You've now zeroed in on the best method for keeping customers loyal while ensuring business continuity, profitability, and trust in the long term.

## Conclusion

Don't get me wrong: acquisition is extremely important for any e-commerce business. In fact, you simply need both to truly succeed, as evidenced by the flywheel approach. Where brands fall down, though, is in over-prioritizing acquisition and de-prioritizing retention. It's like grabbing fish in a net with a big hole; there's no fish left to retain.

In the current e-commerce environment, where it's clear that the top 1% are eyeing your brand and angling to grab your customers, email and SMS is clearly the only way to stave off that competition, level the playing field, and create long-lasting customer relationships that will scale your business profitably.

Now that we've established the critical importance of customer retention and how email and SMS excels in achieving it, I'm sure you're excited to find out how to create a truly profitable, predictable, and sustainable revenue stream from email and SMS.

But first, brands need to get rid of all the bad habits and preconceptions we have about email and SMS. Before I unlock our secret email and SMS strategy, I'm going to share why most brands fail at email and SMS so you can remove all roadblocks from your mindset in preparation for success.

ACQUIRE, NURTURE, CONVERT *AND RETAIN* MORE CUSTOMERS WITH OUR FLYWHEEL APPROACH!

---

**Free E-commerce Growth Guide**

If you're an e-commerce brand looking to scale, you'll need a great acquisition and retention strategy. Although this book is dedicated to email, SMS and CRM, we both know the importance paid media plays in acquiring emails, warm leads, and first-time customers. Our free E-commerce Growth Guide will help you orchestrate all your paid media efforts with email & SMS, creating an orchestrated growth engine for your business that will close more sales and reduce your ad spend. You can download our E-commerce Growth Guide for free by visiting HiFlyerDigital.com/growth.

# CHAPTER THREE

## Why Brands Fail at Email & SMS

So far, we've established that Amazon, digitally-native D2C brands, and the top 1% are focused on acquiring your customers and prioritizing retention via email and SMS as a way of keeping them from leaving. And I've shown you the importance of customer loyalty and how email and SMS is the only way to achieve it successfully and profitably.

Yet this client story (out of many) illustrates a major flaw in how brands perceive email. The words alone revealed a major gap in the e-commerce market: most brands fail at running a successful email & SMS strategy.

When I first started dialoguing with my client, JudaicaPlace.com, the owner was adamant that email was essentially dead.

Everywhere he turned, someone complained that they get too many emails or everyone's on Facebook or Instagram these days, or Google is where people start shopping. So, he was focusing most of his marketing efforts on Google search, PPC, Google Shopping, and Amazon. Needless to say, the business was doing fine, but he sensed there was a gap on the retention side. Email, in his view, wasn't the solution, though.

He had a sizable email list and was marketing to them regularly, but revenue never exceeded 1 to 2% of total e-commerce revenue. The marketing assumption was that email is a way of talking to people and, eventually, maybe they'll buy something down the road.

After we chatted and discussed our unique approach to email and SMS, he decided to see if maybe there was life left in his email list. Within 60 to 90 days, his campaigns were segmented and personalized, non-existent automations were turned on, and email was generating 25% of JudaicaPlace.com's total e-commerce revenue. By the end of the year, email revenue was up 352% year over year, and email became his fastest-growing channel.

The realization was quite apparent - email wasn't dead; the relationship between the brand and their customer was what was dead. **Remember this line: it's not about the SIZE of your email list; it's about the relationship you have TO the list.**

Once we jump-started that email relationship, the revenue potential was unlocked.

I've heard variations of this story from numerous clients as I started working with them. In fact, some of the top brands in the world haven't even scratched the surface of their email potential; they hire me to help them unlock it!

So, if e-commerce brands can potentially unlock 300% revenue growth using email and SMS, why do they fail at achieving that potential? Why do brands assume that "email is dead" or "no one checks email" and give up on all that potential revenue?

After speaking with hundreds of brands, brainstorming with the top ESPs worldwide, and speaking at conferences with vendors and marketers, I've identified the top six reasons why brands fail at email and SMS.

## Reason #1: Bad Relationship Building

How does it feel to be sold? To many, a salesperson is the most abhorrent of individuals. They pressure or smooth talk you into buying products or services you don't need. They make you uncomfortable even if you came into the store looking to buy. We attempt to make zero eye contact and cringe when they come over to see how they can help. Most customers know that salespeople are not there to "help" but rather are angling to meet their quota.

If you've ever read the book, *The Ultimate Sales Machine,* by Chet Holmes, which I highly recommend for every business owner to truly understand customer acquisition, Chet clearly outlines one of the major sales flaws: actual selling.

Ironically, in a book all about sales, Chet says, "selling breaks rapport, but education builds it." **Yet most brands are focused on selling their stuff, and they use email to share with the world that they're selling stuff.** You have an email list, so why not sell them some stuff? Forget if they want it; they're on your list so let's sell them.

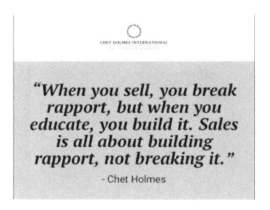

Think about how it feels to be sold. You feel like you're "being talked at" instead of "being connected with." Translating that to email & SMS, **brands are simply "talking at" their customers instead of "communicating with" their customers.** Brands de-prioritize relationship building in favor of selling stuff; that approach breaks rapport and leads to tuning out, disengagement and unsubscribes.

That's reason number one why brands fail at email & SMS: they focus only on selling stuff instead of building relationships.

## Reason #2: Batch & Blast Approach

Going one step deeper, if a brand is motivated to simply sell stuff, then the law of averages kicks in: the more people you can reach at once, the higher likelihood you'll sell the product. In email marketing, this is referred to as "batch and blast" or "spray and pray."

This one-size-fits-all style of marketing is very 1980 and goes against every form of customer-centric, data-driven marketing today. With the data at hand, brands can get highly granular with their marketing segmentation. Yet batch and blast is still a highly recurring trend; surprisingly, even among some of the top 1%!

Think of it this way: if you have revenue goals and KPIs to hit, you need to do everything possible to hit those numbers, so a brute-force attack on your email list sounds very appealing. If you dig deeper, though, you'll find the real reason for batch and blast marketing: lack of marketing strategy or planning. **Simply reading about the Pareto Principle will tell you that mailing to your best people will result in more revenue.**

So, not only do brands use campaign planning inefficiently, they take it out on their customers, blasting them with emails to see what sticks. It's extremely important to remember that behind every email is a person. When that person detects an indifference in how you communicate with them, they opt to churn, unsubscribe, or complain with the spam button.

Those disengaged customers lead to lower customer lifetime value, lower revenue, and more pressure to hit your numbers. That's reason number two for why brands fail at email.

## Reason #3: You're Projecting

We established in the last few chapters that everything revolves around a customer's email or phone number, so it's no wonder that texts get a high click rate, and emails are checked on average 40x a day.

If you think about it, every form of correspondence, both at work and at home, tends to revolve around those two channels. You ask coworkers to "send you an email with the meeting rundown," or you tell your spouse to "text me the grocery list, so I have it," or even encourage home services to "email us your quote." We use email and SMS to communicate about every little thing.

Yet each person has a communication preference. Some prefer email, some like texts, some look forward to mail, and others are phone people. So, those individuals who prefer not to clog up their inbox tend to project their own email experiences and preferences on the channel.

**Number of e-mail users worldwide from 2017 to 2025**
*(in millions)*

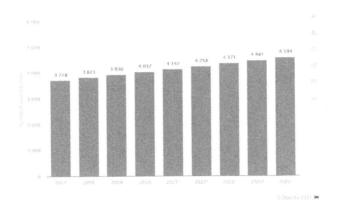

People who can't stand getting too many emails assume that EVERYONE is like them. They posit that since THEY never check their promotions or sales emails, it must be that NO ONE ever checks those emails either. **This leads their brand to neglect the channel and make assumptions about their subscribers.** As shown above, the number of email users is rising, so neglecting the channel will lead to a massive miss for brands that detest getting too much in their inbox.

There's also another type of person who goes 50/50 on email & SMS. These types of people tend to send very few emails, so they don't "spam their list," clearly projecting their own experience on the channel yet again. Every unsubscribe bothers them, so they go entirely hands-off on their program, even though others have indicated a preference to hear from their brand often.

**In this case, they miss 100% of the shots they don't take; revenue doesn't happen unless you start emailing.** This method of sparse marketing could also lead to deliverability problems when they do opt to send an email.

Projecting your personal email experience on the channel and on your full subscriber base is why brands fail at email & SMS.

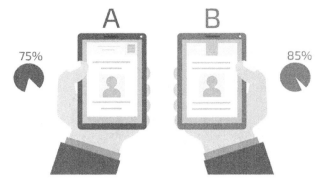

## Reason #4: Zero Focus on A/B Testing

In the startup world, there's a project management process called the Lean Methodology. In short, the Lean Methodology is a way of optimizing the people, resources, effort, and energy of your organization toward creating value for the customer. The way startups achieve that is through a cycle of build-measure-learn, a term coined by Eric Ries in his book, *The Lean Startup*.

I can speak for hours on the process, but here it is in a digestible format: the fastest growing brands in the world get their product out to market fast, measure results, get feedback from customers, and learn from the insights, thereby creating a better product or idea. They test, learn and refine. Note how this is yet another flywheel approach startups love, seeing a trend here in how brands scale fast?

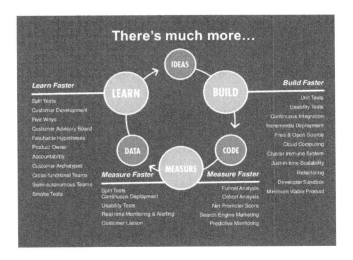

**Most brands, when it comes to email and SMS, put limited to zero focus on learning or A/B testing. And, as you can see from above, if you're not testing, you're not learning.** In some cases, if they actually do some A/B testing, the test isn't very scientific or limited in scalability, which leads to empty conclusions.

Case-in-point: A/B testing the subject line of a single Memorial Day campaign doesn't exactly help you increase open rates for a Black Friday campaign. They are two different times of year, different promotions, different audiences, and different strategies.

I have a great example of the power of testing. Our client, a multi-billion-dollar e-commerce brand, decided to start testing subject lines and template layouts to measure incrementality. Before we even analyzed the results, their brand saw a 30% lift in revenue simply because they implemented testing!

After one campaign, the revenue lift alone justified the "risk" of testing (why brands think testing is a risk is beyond me) and led to further ideas, insights, and inspiration. The best part: the culture of the company shifted to a testing culture instead of merely an order-taking one.

If brands don't test how best to communicate with their customers, they don't learn and refine the dialogue. The result is an underperforming channel and indifferent subscribers; that's why brands fail at email & SMS.

## Reason #5: Non-Linear Customer Journey

Check out your most recent campaign statistics. Did your customers buy the products you were promoting in the email, or did they veer off and buy a bunch of different items?

Email, like Google and Facebook ads, affiliate relationships, and content marketing, is a traffic generator. Good marketers get great traffic from email; great marketers get great conversions from email.

**But customers tend to buy items that they're interested in, not just what you're selling them. The customer journey is simply not linear.**

For that reason, brands throw their hands up in the air and say that email doesn't work because subscribers didn't buy what they were promoting, blaming their results on their subscribers.

The real blame is on their marketing philosophy. You'll learn later on that email and SMS comes down to sending the right person the right message at the right time and repeating it over and over.

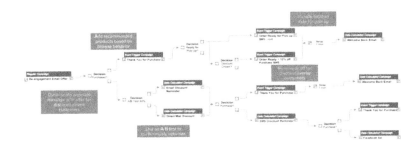

By focusing on segmentation and personalization, brands will learn IF they have an audience for the promotion and IF it's worth promoting.

For everyone else, subscribers will buy whatever they're in the market for at this current time. So, the path to purchase is simply not linear.

Subscribers may get an email and decide to buy something else within the email or something else that may have jogged their memory. Brands need to accept that and realize that email is a traffic generator as well. For brands that expect a 100% DIRECT correlation between product emails and product sales every time is why they fail at email & SMS.

## Reason #6: Social Media is Sexier

Mirror, mirror on the wall, who's the fairest of them all? The brand with the most likes and shares, of course!

**Email and SMS is simply not as sexy as social media.** Opens and clicks aren't as "cool" as likes, retweets, views, and shares. Kudos to social media; we've all been trained in a true Pavlovian manner to base our entire self-worth on vanity metrics.

Between people screaming that "email is dead," brands sharing Facebook ads all over our feeds, and influencers hawking products to millions of followers, it's no wonder that email & SMS gets overlooked.

Quick stats from OptinMonster: even if social media is more prominent in our lives, the channel converts abysmally. The statistics below are pretty generous; the top 1% of brands in the world experience ridiculously low conversion rates from social media. But they know that - which is why they run ads to their site with one goal: **capture emails & phone numbers to convert visitors into customers.**

There are no email forwards or referrals that brands can share with the public, but a like or comment is visible to the world! Vanity metrics look great to everyone, so I can certainly understand the appeal. I also look at our posts, videos, and podcast statistics and smile at every metric. But, for us, email and SMS converts leads into customers.

Neglecting the email and SMS channel for vanity metrics on social media is an easy way to lose sales. Vanity metrics is reason number six why brands fail at email and SMS.

***

Let's recap. I've established why customers leave you for competitors, and I've shown that a strong email and SMS strategy is the best way to combat it. Simultaneously, email and SMS helps level the playing field between you and the top 1% and builds revenue streams that are profitable, predictable, and sustainable. This chapter helped you identify the "bad habits" and preconceived notions about email and SMS and get you thinking about how to break free from those habits going forward.

For most brands, though, the urgency isn't quite there. For some brands, the lack of a strong email and SMS strategy is merely an opportunity they haven't seized yet and haven't truly felt the pain of customer churn. For others, losing customers is a critical problem they needed to solve yesterday. Stop and think: which category does your brand fall under?

Because some brands are constantly in the weeds of the business due to the pandemic and haven't stepped out to see the forest from the trees, the next chapter specifically addresses why establishing a strategic email & SMS plan is critical right here and now.

**Subscribe to our Ecom 80/20 Podcast!**

Subscribe to the e-commerce podcast created for brands who want to compete to win in a crowded marketplace. Hosted by Isaac Hyman and Yaakov Rosenberg, we talk about how e-commerce brands can work smarter, not harder, and build better customer relationships that scale their business. With special guests that include e-commerce founders, e-commerce marketing experts and tech vendors, discover why the 80/20 rule and being customer-centric is critical to ecommerce! You can listen to our past podcast episodes by visiting HiFlyerDigital.com/podcast or subscribing within your preferred podcast listening platform.

# CHAPTER FOUR

## Why Email & SMS is Critical Now

I'm a big fan of Home Goods. Every time I go to the local mall and peruse the aisles of Home Goods, I feel like I'm on a treasure hunt, discovering all types of unique items in every department.

I can actually understand why, as of the writing of this book, they don't have a true e-commerce operation; how can they truly replicate the in-store shopping experience online? There are about three Home Goods locations within 10 miles of my home, and each one has a unique selection.

I guess my love for discovering unique treasures rubbed off on my family. One day, my son, Ben, walked into my office and showed me a recent Home Goods find during his recent trip to the mall. It was a snow globe with "The Office" brand, one of my favorite shows ever.

Similar to the one on Michael Scott's desk, Ben thought this would be a perfect gift for me. Coming from a nine-year-old, this was a very thoughtful gift and adorns my desk to this day.

This snow globe gift has even more meaning to me than just being a wonderful treasure. I co-founded HiFlyer Digital during the pandemic, one of the most challenging times I'll probably ever know. Everything we traditionally knew about the work world - in-office work, stable jobs, 9 to 5 work schedules, and on - were disrupted. The tranquility and consistency of our world were shaken and stirred.

As I've mentioned before, the world, in essence, had become a snow globe. Just like a shaken snow globe upends the snowflakes within, the entire world had been thrown into upheaval nearly overnight. That snow globe that Ben gifted me was a perfect metaphor for why email & SMS is critical right now. Let's take each reason one by one.

## Reason #1: The COVID-19 Snowglobe

The world is like a snow globe right now. Referencing the McKinsey study once again: 76% of consumers have changed buying habits entirely due to COVID-19, pivoting to brands they never tried and leaving brands that they used to be loyal to. Shaken and stirred. In fact, most shoppers are unsure of where they go next - stick with the brands they pivoted to or go back to their traditional habits?

Like a snow globe, the snowflakes - aka customers - are still falling to the ground and finding a place to settle. E-commerce has grown by about 44% in 2020 and is on track to grow by about another 30% in 2022, proving that many customers prefer to maintain their new habits.

The key takeaway is this: customers are still up in the air right now and deciding which brands, products, and experiences they want to stick with post-pandemic. **This once-in-a-lifetime opportunity to grab those customers before they settle into their post-pandemic habits is huge.** One question remains: are you in a position to keep the customers you gained, grab the customers who have pivoted and maintain their loyalty after the pandemic?

**Let's make this point 100% clear: Amazon and the top 1% are extremely well-positioned to grab those customers.** If you're not in a position to grab all those snowflakes, you may squander the largest customer acquisition opportunity you'll ever experience. The window is closing, the snowflakes are settling, and the top 1% are positioning themselves to grab as many customers as they can. If you want to compete post-pandemic, elevating your customer retention strategy is critical now.

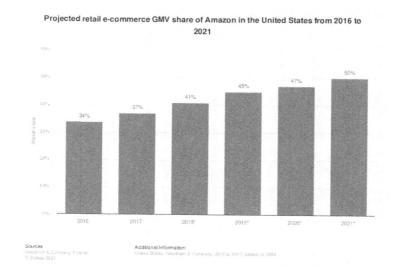

Projected retail e-commerce GMV share of Amazon in the United States from 2016 to 2021

## Reason #2: Amazon's Dominance

I've talked about Amazon extensively in previous chapters, but it's highly important to highlight this: Amazon is consistently three to five years ahead of you.

**The one area Amazon didn't prepare for, like all of us, was a pandemic.** Although their dominant flywheel is grabbing customers away from you left and right during this challenging time, you have a unique window where the playing field is slightly even.

In a disconnected world, customers are craving a human touch, a story, a hero, and a brand they connect with. Although Amazon checks every box on customer shopping convenience, you have an opportunity to build a relationship with customers on a deeper, self-actualization level.

But the window is closing. Amazon has deep pockets to acquire D2C brands, they are focused on creating better brand trust, and they can afford to invest billions into story-telling. If they close that gap, Amazon will absorb more of your customers post-pandemic.

The time to compete is now, while the playing field with Amazon is still somewhat level. Your brand won't find many other opportunities. Building a connected relationship in a disconnected, faceless e-commerce world is critical now.

## Reason #3: Apps = Middlemen

In chapter two, we've established that apps and direct-to-consumer brands are inserting themselves between you and your customer.

**What you need to know is this: apps now have all the information they need, and they're soon going to be pressured to profit from it.**

Let's take Peloton: they accelerated quickly during the pandemic and now, as 2022 began, quickly stumbled due to a misforecast on product demand. Peloton quickly learned that the demand from pandemic customers isn't the same after the pandemic craze subsided, and they're now under pressure to maintain revenue goals before people go back to the gym.

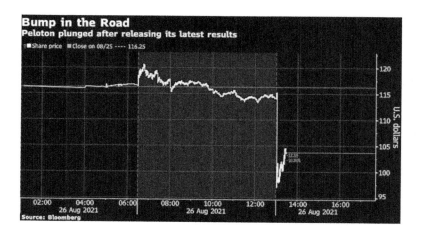

DoorDash and UberEats are in a similar predicament. Remote workers, who relied on these apps for quick delivery in a restricted restaurant sit-down environment, will soon be returning to the office and their beloved lunchtime routines.

Going "back to normal" means fewer customers ordering via app and preferring to walk a few blocks to their favorite lunch place. That means DoorDash and UberEats will need to find new ways to monetize their newly acquired customers as well as raise their fees and percentages from restaurants.

**For these apps, there's one path forward: monetizing their existing customers with a solid customer retention strategy.** Peloton, ShopRunner, DoorDash, UberEats, and more will prioritize retention over acquisition these next few years, trying to extract more revenue from their base through upsells, value offerings, and loyalty programs. New offers to increase customer lifetime value, customer loyalty programs, and financing offers will pop up, and your brand will be forced to compete with all these new value propositions.

AMERICA'S
# DELIVERY APP MARKET

America's food delivery market has boomed in recent years. Here's a look at the biggest players in the space, and how their market share has changed over the last few years.

U.S. Monthly Market Share

100%

75%

**DOORDASH**

DoorDash has captured the largest share of the U.S. delivery app market.

The app is especially popular in San Jose, where it makes up 77% of the market.

50%

Uber Eats

Postmates

25%

Two years ago, Grubhub was accused of charging restaurants fees for calls that never became orders. Since then, the company's market share has dwindled.

**GRUBHUB**

OTHER

0

2018    2019    2020    2021

Source: McKinsey & Company

**One of the most likely outcomes from these apps will be retail media networks**; essentially, this means advertising options for the brands and stores selling on their platform. Take UberEats: they have hundreds of thousands of restaurants on their platform and can now extract advertising dollars from every restaurant. ShopRunner can monetize the retailers on their network and position top spenders higher than brands like yours. These media networks will help apps get a quick cash injection and monetize their customers while potentially positioning you lower than their advertisers in search results.

Apps have inserted themselves between you and the customer, and now, as the pandemic subsides, you're facing an uphill battle to win those customers back to your brand. The e-commerce brands that will win are the ones who act now and create a rock-solid customer retention plan before the apps kick off their value stacking, media networks, and loyalty programs.

## Reason #4: Rising Paid Media Costs

In terms of ad dollars, the law of supply and demand dictates that the more brands bid on your typical advertising keywords, the higher the price Google, Bing, and other search engines can demand. **Since thousands of brands pivoted to or invested in e-commerce during the pandemic, the demand far exceeds the supply; therefore, ad budgets will need to rise quickly.**

If you remember from the previous chapters as well, direct-to-consumer brands have larger war chests and can afford to outspend you. The result is higher ad costs and lower margins as your cost-per-acquisition goes up. Your ad dollars are stretched thinner if you factor in the inflationary economy we're currently in as well. Acquiring a customer will become quite pricey in 2022 and beyond.

**Ironically, though, having a data-driven, customer-centric retention plan will actually help your acquisition efforts.** As we've discussed before, you can take your VIP customers, send their data over to Google and Facebook, create lookalike audiences just like your VIP customers, and run ads to them.

Compare the return-on-ad-spend (ROAS) for those ads vs. running your typical ads; the return will be significantly higher.

Here's another example: pull your unsubscribed list, send that to Facebook, run a win-back campaign to those customers, and get them back as customers or signups. All these acquisition strategies require a retention plan that identifies customers and their lifetime value.

Unless your items are high AOV and your margins are superb, most brands won't be able to weather the ad cost increase.

Considering customer acquisition can never be off the table, offsetting the rise in low-ROI acquisition costs with a high-ROI retention strategy becomes even more important now.

## Reason #5: Cheaper to Retain than Gain

Piggybacking on the rise of acquisition costs, investing in a customer retention strategy goes beyond ad dollars and cents. Even when COVID-19 ends, or if Amazon decides to hang it all up, or even if paid media decreases in cost, there's one constant that still remains.

**It costs 600% more to acquire a customer than it costs to retain one.** From a conversion point of view, existing customers convert 67% of the time while new customers convert 13% of the time. The ROI is all in retention, not acquisition.

I always tell our clients that I tend to strip ideas down to the basics. I ask them to explain their challenges to me like I'm a five-year-old. Sometimes when you think about how to explain complex strategies to kids, you realize that some ideas are extremely simple to understand.

A great example of this is the cart abandon email. Every client asks me if our team will help them with cart abandon and site abandon, and everything abandon. Considering we're the experts in email and SMS, turning on abandon automations is a given. But the real question that any five-year-old would ask is why they are abandoning them in the first place. That's the REAL challenge to fix.

Acquisition is another one that needs to be understood from a basic level. Most brands think that a great marketing strategy entails a paid search, paid social and retargeting plan.

**Here's how we look at it: you're paying Google and Facebook to drive traffic to your website... and then paying Google and Facebook to bring them back to your website when they leave.** Question: what are you doing to keep them there and capture their data, if not their sale? Seems like all brands are doing is making Google and Facebook rich.

Focusing on acquisition, paid search, and retargeting avoids the main issues you should be focusing on: converting customers when they come to your site and growing their value after they sign up and buy.

The urgency to refocus on retention becomes even more pressing when you realize that 74% of customers are one-time buyers; the potential to grow those customers is often overlooked yet has immense profit potential.

So, while your brand keeps gifting Google and Facebook your hard-earned dollars, you're simultaneously leaving customer value untapped and unrealized. That potential alone should strike a sense of urgency in your marketing right now.

*** 

The need to have a solid customer retention strategy powered by email and SMS is critical now. With Amazon's dominant flywheel stealing customers, apps inserting themselves as middlemen, and declining return-on-ad-spend (ROAS), the importance of email and SMS is more urgent than ever.

Let's do a final recap of the challenges, opportunities, and importance of having an email and SMS strategy in place. We've established why customers leave brands for competitors and why email and SMS will keep them loyal. We then focused on why most brands fail at email and SMS, even though it's critical for brands to get it right at this point in time.

Now, the final question remains: how does your brand get it right and create better customer relationships that unlock huge amounts of revenue and profits? And how can your brand turn email and SMS into the most profitable, predictable, and sustainable revenue stream?

We've officially arrived at the strategy phase, what we call our S.P.A.M. Strategy. What I'm about to share with you is the exact blueprint that the top 1% use to drive their business forward, unlock immense revenue streams, build profitable customer lifetime value and scale faster than their competitors.

In order to implement this strategy, let's first ensure you have the building blocks in place to achieve success in email and SMS.

**Subscribe to our Youtube Channel**

From our daily minute-long videos to our in-depth video webinars, our YouTube channel has it all. Forrester Research estimates one minute of online video equates to approximately 1.8 million written words; that means you'll learn a ton about e-commerce and customer retention when you subscribe to our YouTube channel! Watch our latest videos at HiFlyerDigital.com/youtube or subscribe directly on Youtube.

# CHAPTER FIVE

## Building Your Email & SMS Foundation

As we're about to embark on sharing the secret email and SMS strategies of the top 1%, let's do a pre-launch check.

There's nothing worse than getting excited about a new strategy, gearing up to launch it, and then discovering a major roadblock. Maybe you realize that you don't have the right infrastructure in place, data is totally out of sync, or you don't have the deliverability reputation to succeed.

I'll be the first to tell you: I know what that's like! During my time as Director of CRM, our management team came up with tons of ideas, strategies, and tactics. We used to sit in a room offsite for two full days and whiteboard out a full email, SMS and CRM strategy, start to finish.

Being relatively new to the role, I was entirely on board and excited to jump in with my ideas and perspectives. We orchestrated an amazing post-purchase strategy, welcome series, win-back series, nurture program, and upsell/cross plan for our main brand and four sister brands.

After the offsite, we began the project management part of the plan. Here's where we started hitting some bumps in the road. Apparently, we didn't have mission-critical data coming into our ESP in real-time. I also discovered that some important customer insights weren't coming in at all; they were never scoped to be brought into our ESP. That would set the project back a few weeks.

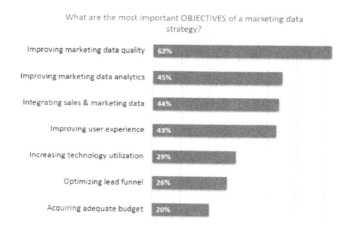

What are the most important OBJECTIVES of a marketing data strategy?

| | |
|---|---|
| Improving marketing data quality | 62% |
| Improving marketing data analytics | 45% |
| Integrating sales & marketing data | 44% |
| Improving user experience | 43% |
| Increasing technology utilization | 29% |
| Optimizing lead funnel | 26% |
| Acquiring adequate budget | 20% |

While we waited for the data requests to be scoped, approved, and implemented, we began modeling some post-purchase segments to ensure they matched with our audience projections. The counts were wildly inaccurate; the raw data showed 200,000 subscribers who bought a certain brand, but the segment counts in our ESP were 30,000. Big red flags shot up.

We didn't have a SQL expert on staff, but I knew the basics like building SQL queries. I used to spend all day trying to figure out why the counts were so wildly inaccurate. There was a time when my CMO even rolled up his sleeves and whipped out his SQL skills, spending half the day on SQL queries, and the counts were still bizarrely inaccurate.

We came to the conclusion that if we planned on implementing the cutting-edge strategies that would help us level up our brand, we would need a new ESP and a full audit of our entire tech stack. You can hear the Debbie Downer groan from here.

My hope for you is that you don't run into the same hard-stop experiences. If I'm going to share the exact strategy of the top 1%, I want to make sure you have the right tools to implement it right away. There's nothing worse than stifling the momentum you get after a great book, webinar, conference, or mastermind session.

So, let's start with a brief overview of the basic building blocks of a successful email and SMS program for e-commerce brands. Side note: if you do feel you have your email and SMS foundation set, jump ahead to chapter six. If not, read ahead!

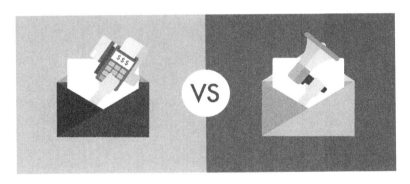

## Promotional vs. Transactional

Most likely, you've heard from your IT team or your ESP vendor that you need to separate your transactional and promotional emails. But what does it mean to separate your emails? Which emails qualify for separation? And is this truly a necessary step?

Before we go too far, let's define what the differences are and how they play a role in email marketing. You can lump most email messages into two camps—promotional and transactional. Here's what we mean when we use these terms.

**Promotional emails**

A promotional email (also called a batch mailing, BAU email, broadcast, or bulk email) is an email that is sent to more than one person that contains the exact same content and is not triggered by an event. A promotional email would be anything a customer did not specifically trigger, for example, a weekly newsletter, a marketing email, or an announcement about your site's recent updates.

### Transactional emails

Transactional emails are emails that the customer triggers. An order confirmation email after a customer places an order, an alert email a customer has set up in your app, and an account signup email all qualify as transactional emails.

Remember when I mentioned that I need things explained to me like a five-year-old sometimes? **This is how I'd explain promotional vs. transactional to a five-year-old: a transactional email is an email that a customer EXPECTS to receive while a promotional email isn't.**

A lost password email, order confirmation email, notify me when in stock email, and an account signup email are examples of emails that someone expects to receive. They've opted to "trigger" this email and expect that email in their inbox.

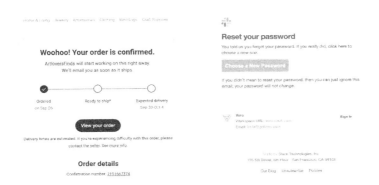

A promotional email is an email that one doesn't necessarily expect. A sale email, last chance promo email, or cart abandon email isn't always expected. Yes, they've opted in to hear from you, yet these are more sales-oriented. For that reason, these are considered promotional emails.

There are definitely gray areas. Take a review solicitation email, for example; it's related to your transaction, but the review submission goal is closer to promotional. As such, you may need to define what these mean to your business and measure how customers react to each type of email.

Because transactional emails are expected while promotional emails aren't always, promotional emails have lower engagement rates. Average open rates for promotional campaigns hover between 10-20%. That's much lower than the 70% open rates that are typical for transactional emails. Engagement impacts sender reputation, and you wouldn't want lower engagement on batch emails to affect the delivery of critical transactional messages.

I won't go into all the specifics of how to optimize your promotional or transactional emails in this chapter - such as subdomains, IP address, new email address, etc. - as this is just an explanation of the differences between the two types of emails. In a later chapter, I'll share some of the revenue opportunities that exist within transactional emails.

## Email Service Provider (ESPs)

If you're reading this book, you most likely have a good grasp of what an ESP does. But not every brand understands the tiers of ESP out there and tends to think that Klaviyo, Mailchimp, or OmniSend are the best options in the market.

This section will give you some ideas to consider as you use those entry-level ESPs and vet larger ones as you scale. And for those who are just starting out, here's a quick primer on the importance of an e-commerce ESP and what you need to know before you select one.

ESPs – Email Service Providers – are email marketing and distribution services for your business. They can be integrated into your CRM or CMS to work seamlessly with your email list.

ESPs make managing your email lists, collecting new email addresses, and analyzing email marketing campaigns simple.

Choosing the right ESP will optimize your deliverability rates, your open rates, and ultimately lead to more sales. ESPs will make it easy for you to customize your email marketing to different target segments within your audience. They'll also help you ensure you're complying with laws regarding marketing and spam.

With so many options available, here are a few things to consider when choosing the right ESP for you:

- **Deliverability** is the likelihood that your emails will reach your subscribers' inbox. Email Tool Tester recently did some research on which ESP has the best deliverability, and here are the results:

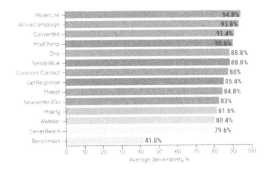

- **Security:** Your ESP should give you peace of mind that your customers' data will be secure. Look into aspects such as password policies, encryption safeguards, and the use of firewalls. With GDPR, CCPA, and other privacy regulations being enacted, it's extremely important to choose an ESP with thorough security standards for the sake of your customers.

- **Reporting and Analytics:** The reporting your ESP provides can help you adjust and improve on the performance of future campaigns. But you might want a more comprehensive analysis of data such as where your subscribers are located, the devices used to open your mail, and click maps, which show you how your audience is interacting with your email content. You will eventually want more predictive analytics and machine learning as well as you scale your brand. Think about which metrics you want to track and ensure you choose an ESP that supports this.

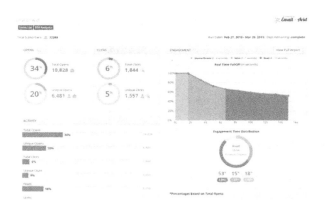

- **Integrations:** Most ESPs offer integrations with major CMS, CRM, e-commerce apps, and platforms. At the very least, they should have APIs or plugins that you can use to build custom integrations. Consider how much implementation, training, and management is required to get you or your team set up with the new ESP, as well as the costs to hire a dev team to get you up and running seamlessly.

- **Overall Strategy:** When choosing the right ESP, it's helpful to have a clear idea of what your email marketing strategy will look like. For example, if you're a blog, you'll need an ESP that excels in content marketing using feeds; if you're an e-commerce store, you'll need to send marketing emails with updated product data. In addition, identifying the email types - newsletters, promotions, workflows, triggers, lifecycle campaigns, and on - will help you kick the tires better. Knowing exactly what you require and how you want your strategy to play out will give you the best chance of choosing the right ESP for your needs.

- **Out-of-the-box features:** Once you've mapped out your strategy, the features you require from an ESP will be clearer, and you're able to narrow down the platforms that provide the most important tools right away (aka "out of the box!") Ask yourself:
    - Do I want ready-made email templates or the ability to create custom HTML templates?
    - Do I prefer WYSIWYG drag-and-drop builders or intense HTML-coded templates?
    - Do I want an ESP that charges by the number of emails sent or the number of customer profiles in the database? Some even charge based on the number of emails clicked.
    - Do I want an ESP that focuses on email only or one that allows for cross-channel marketing via

SMS, Facebook ads, Google ads, push notifications, and more?

- **Customer Support:** Sometimes, campaigns and flows just don't go according to plan, and you'll need a strong customer support system to get you out of these tricky situations. While all good ESPs should have email and phone support, check for other options like social media support. Another handy function in an emergency is the 24/7 chat function on some sites.

- **Your budget:** This plays the biggest role in deciding which ESP is perfect for your brand. Keep your budget in mind, and know exactly what you're able to afford in an ESP and what you can do without. Make sure you take all additional costs into account, such as dedicated IP addresses, extra features, and data storage. Be sure to check how your ESP calculates price - by CPM or by the number of contacts - and forecast your projected list growth so as not to exceed your budget.

Be sure to think about the long-term ROI of an ESP investment. As a data-driven marketer, I'm always thinking about the potential of new technology and illustrating how the ROI will be there if implemented and utilized correctly.

When I onboarded Bluecore, one of my favorite ESPs, I was sure to check with my close friends and colleagues at Sephora, Jockey, and Teleflora on the projected ROI.

Bluecore's cost-per-click model was a unique model compared to the traditional cost-per-thousand sends we're used to seeing in the industry. So, I needed to be sure I could monetize every single click without going over budget. I had to convince upper management about the value of a CPC-based ESP, but once I did, we quickly saw a huge ROI.

Bluecore helped us grow automation revenue by 300% that year because I took the time to think long-term and ensure I had the right strategy in place. Remember this: technology is just a tool. And that tool is only as good as the strategy and team guiding it.

One final point: be realistic when it comes to which features and extras you'll actually use and those which you can easily do without. Most companies only implement 10% of the technology they buy, which is quite wasteful. Focusing on the core aspects of your ESP and adding on new features slowly is the key to maximizing your ESP investment.

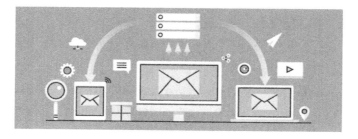

## Email Deliverability 101

A user forgot their password? Send an email with reset instructions. A new product was just launched? Launch a new product email. Traffic on the site is slow this week? Send a roundup of the best-sellers to your mailing list. Companies send emails all the time.

Yet, according to the latest annual research from Return Path, only 85% of legit emails reach their final destination. This means that, on average, every 3 out of 20 users (or a whooping 15,000+ users on a one-million-member list) might abandon your platform, won't know about that shiny new product, or fail to shop during a slow week, bringing revenue down.

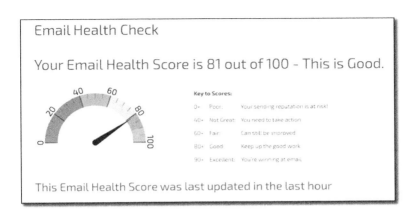

**Email Health Check**

Your Email Health Score is 81 out of 100 - This is Good.

40  60
20        80
0          100

Key to Scores:

0+    Poor:         Your sending reputation is at risk!
40+   Not Great:    You need to take action
60+   Fair:         Can still be improved
80+   Good:         Keep up the good work
90+   Excellent:    You're winning at email

This Email Health Score was last updated in the last hour

As great as your design, content, and creatives may be, if you can't get the email delivered to the inbox, you won't succeed at email marketing. ISPs care a lot about the credibility of your domain and IP address. Before any email is delivered, they'll run a so-called 'reputation check' to evaluate if you're likely to be sending unwanted messages or might have some nefarious motives for contacting your mailing lists. If they deem you do, your deliverability will likely suffer.

The topic of email deliverability is vast, and I'm not going to dive into every specific nuance of deliverability here. What I would recommend is that you use MX Toolbox to run a free deliverability check and see what that tells you about your email program. If there are indeed deliverability issues, enlist the help of your ESP or use MX Toolbox to solve them for you.

What I do want to share, though, is how to ensure strong deliverability going forward. Here are some good deliverability rules to follow:

**Focus on segmentation**

A batch and blast approach is a sure-fire way to have deliverability issues. We have clients who've been sending to their full list in an effort to get subscribers who "may eventually want to buy," which already sounds like a shot in the dark. We quickly walked them back from that approach, using the Pareto Principle as a guide.

Segment out your list by engagement level, purchasing behavior, browsing behavior, and other signals that show a repeated willingness to hear from you. We'll go into more segmentation concepts as I share our unique S.P.A.M. Strategy.

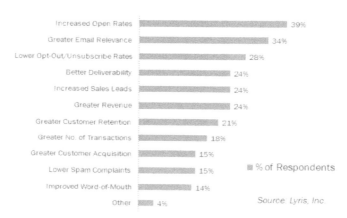

**Email List Segmentation Results**

While buying mailing lists is an obvious no-no, you should also be careful about emailing people who didn't give you explicit permission to do so. Just because someone joined one of your events a year ago or signed up a decade ago doesn't mean they will appreciate being notified about your new product launch.

These "dormant" subscribers are likely to mark your message as spam just to get it out of their inbox. Even a few such requests are enough to significantly harm the reputation of your domain and get you blocked on future mailings.

**Make it super simple to unsubscribe.**

We've had clients that have dreaded the unsubscribe so much that they simply never mail enough. So, having a super-easy method to unsubscribe might sound counterintuitive to certain brands. After all, you've spent time and money building your mailing list, so why would you let them go so easily now?

Check your own inbox. Chances are you're probably subscribed to some mailing lists (voluntarily or not) and hardly ever even open their emails. It could be that you signed up to access some marketing concept, sales funnel, or sampled a product that you have no need for now. We've all done that.

There are thousands of such people on your list, and if they don't interact with you now, there's a minimal chance they will in the future. If you make it hard for them to remove themselves from the list, sooner or later, they'll hit 'SPAM' and quit anyway. What's more, ISPs also look at whether people interact with your emails when assessing your reputation. If they never open them, it won't help your cause.

**Focus on opt-downs, not just opt-outs.**

Subscribers might not necessarily want to unsubscribe from all your communication when they veer to the unsubscribe button.

Chances are they're just receiving too many emails or need a break, or simply are not in the market for your product right now.

An email preference center with opt-in, opt-down, and opt-out options will help you manage your list hygiene. Some brands will even include options to subscribe to new arrivals or content emails over promotions.

Some brands implement a "snooze" function that pauses emails for 30 days. A preference center is a great way to let users decide what they wish to receive and how often, giving them control of their experience.

However, some brands elect to implement super-granular preference centers and drill down deeply into category, interest, location, and other types of email campaigns that users can select to receive. I'll go on the record as saying this is a terrible idea.

One client had a preference center with about 40 checkboxes of product preferences that they could opt-in to hear more about. Add in different communication cadence levels - such as a preference for one email a week or two a month - and the combinations get extremely cumbersome. From a customer point of view, a super granular preference center may look wonderful, but from an email execution perspective, it's a train wreck. Here's an example of a super-granular and cumbersome preference center:

Trying to segment out users who want to hear about pants but not shirts and only want one email a week leads to a super tiny segment and doesn't add any lift to revenue. The sheer number of preference center combinations will cause your team to spend more time segmenting than actually mailing. In my experience, brands with a cumbersome preference center don't really honor it due to time constraints from the email team.

The case for a simple preference center gets even stronger: customers rarely use the preference center anyway. In addition, if they do show an interest in a certain product and buy that product, their preference is outdated because the interest wanes; they've bought the product already, why do they need to hear about it anymore?

We'll discuss later in this book that there are better ways than a preference center to segment subscribers. Your preference center should contain no more than roughly five to seven options:

- Subscribe to all emails
- Subscribe to 1 email roundup a week
- Subscribe to 1 email roundup a month
- Subscribe to breaking news / new products
- Snooze for thirty days
- Unsubscribe

By having opt-down options, you'll reduce the number of unsubscribes while also reducing the preference complexity your email team needs to adhere to.

**Clean your list of disengaged subscribers.**

Letting people unsubscribe easily is not enough. You should also remove some contacts on your own, believe it or not. The obvious case is bounces. If your mailing software doesn't automatically remove accounts that bounce, do it manually. Even several bounces from one campaign can cost you a serious chunk of the good reputation you've earned.

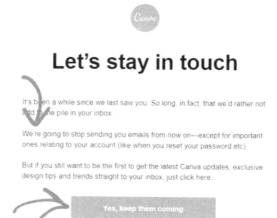

# Let's stay in touch

It's been a while since we last saw you. So long, in fact, that we'd rather not add to the pile in your inbox.

We're going to stop sending you emails from now on—except for important ones relating to your account (like when you reset your password etc).

But if you still want to be the first to get the latest Canva updates, exclusive design tips and trends straight to your inbox, just click here.

Yes, keep them coming

The top e-commerce ESPs like Klaviyo, Sailthru, and Bluecore offer detailed stats for each of your campaigns. You can easily check who opened your emails, who clicked on the links and how many times they did either. This lets you quickly determine who hasn't been active for ages and is just decreasing the quality of your list. Remove such users periodically and focus on those that appreciate your content.

**Avoid spam traps and blacklists**

Spam traps are fake email accounts set up by ISPs and placed in various locations around the web. While harvesting emails, bots also tend to add these addresses to their collections as they look no different than the real accounts bots are after. Send a single email to such an account, and your deliverability will immediately suffer. MX Toolbox has a free tool for checking if your domain has already ended up on one of the blacklists.

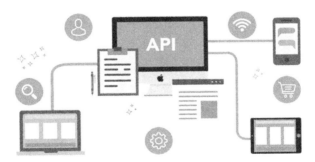

# Third-Party Integrations

When you're deciding which ESP and which CRM to use, think about your future CRM-ESP integration.

CRM-ESP integrations are pivotal to the success of any email marketing program. You can't get the information you'll need to create a strategic email marketing program without the personalization and segmentation data from a CRM.

A CRM (which stands for "customer relationship management") tool is integral for the success of any business, especially E-commerce. Ideally, your CRM will gather your customer interactions across all channels into one platform, enabling you to gain a holistic view of how any given customer has interacted with your brand in any number of ways in one place.

Nowadays, the buzzword for e-commerce brands is CDP - customer data platform - and they act as a "single source of truth" for your customer.

The added value of a CDP is the opportunity to predict customer behavior using bespoke or machine-learning customer modeling as well as push out marketing campaigns directly from their platform.

See the CDP visualization below.

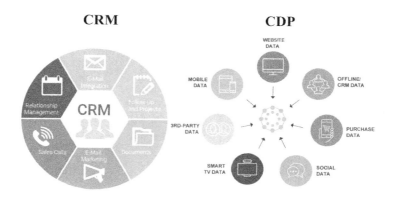

While different CRMs do different things, most CRMs will at the very least keep a record of what a customer purchased from you and when they made that purchase or purchases. Additionally, most CRMs will keep a record of all communications a customer has had with your business over email, chat, SMS, in-store, phone, and beyond.

The point of mentioning a CRM, ESP, and CDP is that you should know what the software you pay for does, what its capabilities are, and how you can get the most bang for your buck by using it to its limit.

More importantly, you can set up a better email marketing program once you've integrated your CRM and your ESP. Better email marketing doesn't just mean that people will like the emails you send more (although that's a great starting goal!) – it often also means a better ROI on your email marketing program.

Integrating your CRM and ESP means you've connected the two platforms, enabling one or both platforms to share data with the other. These days, most ESPs act as a de-facto CRM for e-commerce brands, so the complexity is reduced, and segmentation/personalization is available out of the box.

Having said that, a robust CRM that contains additional customer data that's not found in your ESP can bring your segmentation and personalization to the next level. Take multi-location brick and mortar stores: a CRM with individual store data can greatly benefit your customer segmentation and personalization options within your ESP.

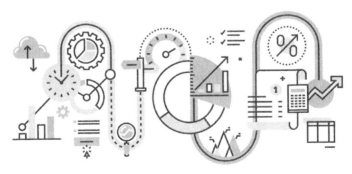

## The Data Essentials & Wishlist

The secret to great email marketing lies in segmentation and personalization. Those two pillars rely on data.

Having data for the sake of data is not enough. As a marketer, you need to turn copious amounts of data from myriad sources into clean, consistent, and actionable data. Let's dive into the core sources of data that your E-commerce business must bring into your email marketing:

- **Purchase data:** No surprise, you need to ensure clean purchase data is coming into your ESP at all times. Some brands prefer daily feeds from their CMS, others prefer real-time purchase data via API, and some have pixel tracking built-in. All have benefits, especially when dealing with fraudulent orders, in-store purchases, returns, or pre-orders. The cleaner the purchase data, the better your email and SMS will perform.

- **Browse data:** Knowing what a subscriber is doing at this very moment is critical for the modern-day marketer. It's not enough to know what a customer HAS shopped, carted, and used; it's more valuable to see what they WILL shop, cart, and buy.

- **Product data**: Clean product data, complete with taxonomy, categorization, attributes, specifications, and stock level will boost your personalization capabilities significantly. There's nothing worse than sending a customer a cart abandon email for a product that's on pre-order or featuring a popular camera to thousands of customers and realizing it's been sold out for months. Your best-performing automations - cart abandon, browse abandon, and post-purchase, to name a few - tend to be product-centric. If the product details, images, and links are rife with errors or outdated quickly, those automations will often fail. Clean product data - complete with a comprehensive data dictionary to understand every data point - is critically important.

- **Customer data**: Creating a customer-centric email program will help you become a truly differentiated, trusted, and successful brand. Customer data goes beyond merely purchase and browse history; think about subscription preferences, credit & financing specifics, loyalty & points, preferred store location, net promoter score, reviews & feedback, and any other data points that will enable you to enrich the customer experience via email and SMS. There may be multiple sources for customer data - especially if you have a reward, credit, and financing setup - so be prepared to have multiple APIs or feed connections powered into your ESP.

- **Engagement data:** Typically, this is part of your ESP - opens, clicks, unsubscribes, site visits, and on - but there are some scenarios where brands will miss opportunities. An example of that would be if a customer visited your store or placed an order in-store; that's an important data piece to bring into your ESP. Another example are SMS and push notifications - knowing if a customer was communicated with via those channels would be helpful so you can suppress them from any additional marketing efforts today. The top brands use their ESP / CRM / CDP as a hub for communication so they don't overwhelm their customers. The value of creating a staggered multi-channel marketing flow is monumental and will help you reduce disengagement and unsubscribes while increasing the chance of a conversion. A sample of a high-performing multi-channel marketing approach, like a cart abandon, could go as follows:
  - ○ Touch 1 - Send email
  - ○ Touch 2 - Send SMS
  - ○ Touch 3 - Send email two

- Touch 4 - Send to Facebook for retargeting

These are the five data pillars you'll need to create a truly magical email, SMS and CRM strategy. Most of your marketing capabilities can be achieved using each of the data points above, but when used alone, each pillar doesn't provide enough value.

Here are a couple examples where missing data causes missed opportunities:

- **Post-Purchase**: Your ESP may see a purchase come in (via pixel tracking) and immediately begin your post-purchase email series. But if the order was canceled or returned a day later and your ESP didn't know about it, that post-purchase email looks kind of ridiculous. And you don't want customer service ringing you up every day with a complaint, trust me!
- **Cart Abandon & Out of Stock Items**: powering a cart abandon series is a great revenue driver. For products that are out of stock (OOS), only on pre-order, or are add-ons to other products, cart abandon emails become very annoying. Creating a suppression for OOS items and pre-orders should be in your product feed.
- **Welcome Series Buyers vs. Non-Buyers:** Triggering a Welcome email to new signups with a discount is great, but what if that new subscriber is a new customer who joined the list at the same time? Triggering a discount to

that customer leads to customer complaints that they want to use that discount on their recently placed order. Cue the headaches. Using your purchase and engagement data, your ESP needs to split the path of a new subscriber and new customer and send slightly different experiences to each.

These examples will illustrate how to orchestrate your data to work together and amplify each other. Remember: the key is to have actionable data, not just all data. It's very appealing to have all your customer data come into your ESP and just cover yourself, but, in my experience, sending all the data leads to slower campaign launches, slower segment building, and an overall sluggish ESP as it tries to wade through all the information. Focus on actionable data, not the most data.

This brings us to the topic of first, second, and third-party data. These terms are essentially sources where you can get all the above data sets powered to your business, ESP or CRM to help enrich your customer profiles or acquire customers.

Here's a quick primer on these data sources and what they mean for your business:

**First-Party Data**

First-party data is essentially data explicitly provided to you by the end-user, such as an email opt-in, SMS opt-in, or address information with purchase. First-party data is highly valuable because of its high quality. Because you collected it directly from the source, you know it's accurate and highly relevant. Privacy concerns are therefore minimal, and, since the access was explicitly granted, you now own the data.

Most customers don't realize this, but when they submit an email or an SMS phone number, they unlock hundreds of additional data points within your tool, such as IP address, browser/device, mobile IDs, online cookies, or other 1s and 0s that can be very hard to sift through.

There are many options for how you can use first-party data. You can use it to predict future patterns of their customers, gain audience insights, and email and SMS personalization. Some of the best personalization occurs with first-party data; think about high-performing birthday automation that gifts a subscriber when their big day nears.

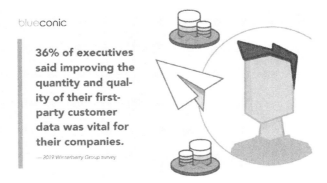

blueconic

**36% of executives said improving the quantity and quality of their first-party customer data was vital for their companies.**

— 2019 Winterberry Group survey

### Second Party Data

Second-party data is essentially someone else's first-party data. The seller collects data straight from their audience, and it all comes from one source. You can feel confident in its accuracy since you're purchasing second-party data directly from a company that owns it. There's no middleman in this transaction; all you need to do is seek out a company with the data you need and form a relationship with them.

Second-party data is similar to first-party data, but it comes from a source other than your own audience. It can include data from many of the same sources first-party data comes from, such as activity on websites, mobile app usage, social media, or customer surveys.

Second-party data helps you stitch together additional insights you couldn't get from first-party data alone. Most e-commerce brands might purchase this type of data to add scale to their first-party data, especially if their first-party data sets are small but growing. And because the data comes directly from a company that collected it, there is transparency between you and the company. This gives you control over what to buy and how the data gets used.

**Better customer experiences require better data.**

First-party data is marketers' top choice for driving customer engagement and insights.

**74%** say first-party data gives the greatest insight into their customers

**64%** say first-party data leads to the highest increase in customer lifetime value

**62%** say first-party data offers the highest lift among data sources

**Less than 10% of marketers** report the same benefits from using third-party data.

An example of second-party data in action would be for a new product line, such as a new men's product for a historically female-centric brand. If you've historically targeted women, you wouldn't have enough data on men to power a truly great launch. As such, you might partner with a men's health, fashion, or fitness website and buy the data you need from them.

Another example is acquiring new leads. Partnering with certain brands that have millions of email addresses and sending targeted emails to their list or even buying those lists and running ads to that list is a great way to acquire leads quickly. As an email marketer, I would personally advise against simply buying email lists and throwing them into your database; you'd have to warm them up and get some form of permission from them before marketing to them within your ESP. In lieu of mass-mailing this new email list, I've found the best approach to leverage social media ads to get their opt-in, thereby turning those users into first-party data.

**Third-Party Data**

Finally, there's a third tier of data. Third-party data is data that you buy from outside sources that are not the original collectors of that data. Instead, you buy it from large data aggregators that pull it from various other platforms or websites that it was generated, such as insurance lists, opt-in forms, medical quotes, and on. These aggregators pay publishers and other data owners for their first-party data. The aggregators then collect into one large data set and sell it as third-party data. Many different companies sell this kind of data, and it is accessible through many different avenues.

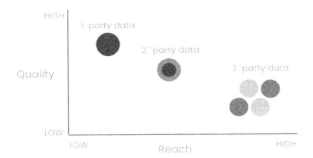

You can use third-party data in the same way as second-party data; the only difference is its cleanliness. You can use it to expand your audiences, enhance your first-party data, and increase the precision of your acquisition ads, helping you discover new audiences.

I'll give a really great example of third-party data working extremely well for cart abandonment. Generally speaking, you can identify maybe 50% of the total cart abandonment on your website. Of that 50%, maybe half or 25% are actually subscribed to your email list. Imagine if you could get that remaining 25% to convert somehow AND also identify the other 50% in some way and try to reach them with a cart abandon! How great would that be for your business!

Here's where a third-party data provider becomes very useful. If that provider can identify those emails or even market to them on your behalf, that would be a very high ROI investment. There are vendors who do exactly that, and we love sharing their information with our clients to increase profits. Third-party data offers some great incrementality to your marketing strategy.

In summary, actionable data is always better. First-party data is critical to a personalized email and SMS strategy, but you can also fill in the gaps or enrich your customer profile using second and third-party data sources.

## Key Performance Indicators (KPIs)

What gets measured gets improved. In the e-commerce world, we use key performance indicators (KPIs) to measure the results of a campaign, trend, customer migration, conversion, and more results-oriented data.

Key performance indicators always go in step with business activities. Only by measuring the effectiveness of your actions can you figure out which of them is best to implement and what has to be discontinued.

To complete our summary of the email, SMS and CRM essentials, I'm outlining the most important email metrics that have to be measured when implementing our strategy. We'll also be looking at how to measure and improve them because every email marketing metric here has a purpose, and each metric must be improved.

In addition, I'll highlight some of the additional CRM KPIs, which measure customer lifecycles and migrations. Not every brand is ready to start measuring these, but it's helpful to know how to track and capitalize on customer lifetime value.

For every KPI, there's an industry-wide benchmark you can use to show where you are and where you want to be. I'll list the latest benchmarks in each relevant KPI below.

## Conversion Rate

This is the most important KPI in email marketing. Quite obviously, all your marketing activities are aimed at increasing sales. Conversion rate (CVR) generally measures how many of your contacts ended up completing checkout. This is the number of sales made from a particular campaign, divided by the number of emails sent and multiplied by 100.

| Email Type | Open Rate | Click-Through Rate | Conversion Rate |
|---|---|---|---|
| Newsletter | 23.40% | 17.80% | 1% |
| Order Follow-Up | 46.10% | 16.70% | 5% |
| Inactive Customers | 38.90% | 19.50% | 2.60% |
| Abandoned Cart | 46.60% | 28.70% | 5% |
| Member Follow-Up | 39.20% | 22.40% | 2.70% |

For example, if a campaign is sent to 10,000 subscribers and generates 300 orders, then CVR would be 300/10,000 * 100 = 3% (this is your conversion rate).

Now, this example is a great CVR; the average CVR for email is about 2%, and that's only if you're achieving great segmentation and personalization. Workflows and automations can yield a higher CVR in the range of 3% to 5% because they're timely and relevant.

In order to optimize for conversion rate, run your flows for 30 days to get a baseline. Then make a few adjustments to your recommendations, banners, or postcards, and A/B test it. That will help you see how well you can increase CVR. Of course, the website plays the most important role in converting, so conversion rate optimization should be explored once you've hit your ceiling on CVR (different book for a different time!)

**Email Opt-In Rate (Conversion Rate)**

But in some cases, conversion rate refers to another action. For example, if you're trying to measure email signups, the "conversion" rate would be more related to lightbox displays vs. lightbox signups. The average newsletter signup rate is around 2%. This means that only 2% of all website visitors enter their addresses to get on your mailing list.

The top 10% of e-commerce stores get an average 4.77% signup rate, so there's always room for improvement if you have a low opt-in rate.

**Email ROI**

By calculating the return on investment or ROI in email marketing, we can evaluate the effectiveness of your email marketing investment. Basically, retailers determine what they gained from the investment in email marketing and how much they spent on it.

The return on email marketing investment formula is as follows:

$$\text{Email Marketing ROI} = \frac{\text{Gain} - \text{Costs}}{\text{Costs}} \times 100$$

**Gain:** the amount of money you earned from email marketing activities
**Costs:** the amount of money you spent on email marketing resources

In this formula, what you earn is the sum of all sales made through email campaigns, automated workflows, etc., over a certain period of time. It doesn't really focus on the number of emails you've sent.

Expenses include the email service fee plus the salaries of email marketers, designers, and other people who helped to implement your email marketing plan over the same period of time.

However, it can sometimes be difficult to come up with a definite price for the time spent on designing emails, writing copy, picking the right products, etc. If you don't have specific numbers, your ROI can become inaccurate.

For that reason, many e-commerce marketers measure more tangible things, such as the ROI for their email marketing tool.

To do so, you simply add up your revenue over the month, subtract the monthly email service fee and divide this number by the amount of money spent on the monthly email service fee.

For example:

Let's say from email marketing campaigns and automated workflows, you earned $20,500 last month, and your monthly fee for Klaviyo was $228.

$(20,500 - 228)/228 = 88.9$

So, for every $1 spent on Klaviyo, you earned $88.90. If you do most of the email marketing work on your own, this measure is more accurate than measuring ROI.

**Click-Through Rate**

The click-through rate refers to how many email recipients clicked on at least one link within the email campaign. This metric is also one of the top email marketing metrics that email service providers indicate in their reports. **As you'll see later in this book, I believe an email click is the most important area to track because every relationship starts with a click. If subscribers don't click with you, there's no relationship.**

$$CTR = \frac{Clicks}{Impressions} \times 100$$

In most ESPs, all the clicks can be seen in the click map in your campaign report. A click map helps a lot when you try to understand what parts of the email are effective and what should be improved. These click maps count the unique (unique clicks on the different links) as well as total clicks (all the clicks, including multiple clicks from the same recipient).

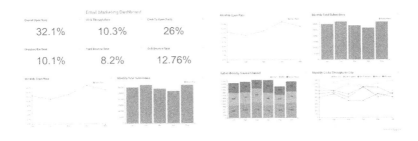

Your click rate indicates how compelling your email content is to its recipients. This includes copy, creatives, content, and how clear and actionable the CTA (call to action) buttons were.

# C-4 DESIGN PLAYBOOK

When it comes to maximizing your click rate, we employ our unique C-4 Design Playbook. You may recognize C-4 as the plastic explosive from major action movies. It's a fitting tongue-in-cheek analogy that shows how our four pillars of design "explode" your clicks and conversions.

I'll deep dive into the C-4 Design Playbook in chapter nine but, considering we're talking about KPIs, here's a quick glance:

- **Pillar 1: Context** - I'm a big fan of great copy because the best writers are experts at persuasion. You can only use sale, last chance, extended and limited stock so many times before your emails get stale. And who wants to always be on discount all the time? But copy alone is not enough; you need to have the right context that shows what your product, offer, or service does for the subscriber. You need to accentuate WHY the product is great for your customer and helps benefit their life. Add in an offer to the mix, and you've got context covered.

- **Pillar 2: Creatives** - like any restaurant will tell you, diners eat with their eyes first. The same goes for email and SMS creatives; they need to be designed to capture the essence of your context. Every creative has one goal: to visually illustrate your context, message, and offer... and achieve the next critical element in the C-4 Design Playbook.
- **Pillar 3: Click** - every relationship starts with a click. Think about how Google and Facebook rose to become advertising behemoths: pay-per-click. When a user clicks, showing high intent, a huge amount of data, intent, and personalization are unlocked. Your creatives can be gorgeous, your copy could be expertly written, and your context could be really dialed in; if your creatives, though, aren't designed to be clicked, you've wasted a lot of energy. Make your email scannable and actionable with a click. The click is all that matters when it comes to email & SMS.
- **Conversion** - finding the right destination URL is just as important as getting the click. Have a great linking strategy in place and use your website's full potential. Linking a New Arrivals email to a category listing page (CLP) won't convert as well as linking a product-listing page (PLP) that has one-click add to cart functionality. Another example of a great linking strategy is utilizing your product filters, sorting, and refinements to help users get to a super-specific set of products or a certain SKU, like a red camera instead of a black camera. Sending the right message to the right person at the right time -and to the RIGHT PLACE - will help you convert

more sales each time. The link plays a hugely important role in converting.

**Bounce Rate**

In email marketing metrics, bounce rate refers to the percentage of your emails that failed to reach their destination. Unlike a website bounce which measures how many people came to your site and made the decision to walk right out, an email bounce indicates that something prevented an email from reaching a recipient's inbox.

There are two different types of bounces, soft bounce and hard bounce, and the differences are here:

- a recipient has a full inbox (soft bounce)
- a recipient has an out-of-office message (soft bounce)
- the email address no longer exists (hard bounce)
- the domain (email ending after @) does not exist (hard bounce)
- the server is not accepting emails (hard bounce)

- the address is mistyped (name@example.cam instead of name@example.com, etc.) (hard bounce)

A soft bounce isn't too concerning as these are usually temporary issues; most ESPs will flag a soft bounce and try up to three emails before marking the recipient as a hard bounce.

With hard bounces, most ESPs will simply remove hard bounces automatically. No ESP wants a hard bounce to affect their deliverability, especially on a shared IP.

On average, a .5% bounce rate for e-commerce brands is normal, while a bounce rate greater than 4% can damage your sender's reputation. If you see your bounce rate creeping out, start cleaning your list to ensure your IP address remains reputable.

**Spam Rate**

The dreaded spam rate is one of the most important KPIs to monitor closely. Your spam rate refers to how many people find your emails annoying or irrelevant. Essentially, individuals are flagging your emails as spam. Not cool.

People will hit the spam button, though, so 0.1% is a reasonable spam rate. Anything more than that needs to act as a red flag, causing you to rethink and clean your email list. A big complaint rate might spoil your sender's reputation, which means that your future emails will not be delivered to recipients.

The solution for dropping the spam rate is segmentation and personalization. Send fewer emails to the unengaged and better emails to the engaged. Using the strategy I'll show you in the next chapter, I've been able to send 40% fewer emails while increasing revenue by 50% simply due to segmentation and personalization; an added bonus was dropping our spam rate and unsubscribe rate as well.

**Unsubscribe Rate**

Fact: people will unsubscribe, and that's not always a bad thing. It's heartbreaking, but that's okay. It happens to all e-commerce brands and retailers.

The average unsubscribe rate for e-commerce is about 0.25%. So, you shouldn't worry about unsubscribes unless you get a significantly higher rate of declines. Most brands should feel totally fine if their unsubscribe rate is lower than 0.90%, but anything over 1% is a red flag.

Unsubscribes occur for numerous reasons, including:

- Your emails are too frequent
- Your emails aren't personalized
- The email list is stale itself.
- Your emails aren't informative, helpful, or educational

Similar to the spam rate, our strategy will help you bring down the unsubscribe rate as well.

**Open Rate**

To me, open rates were always kind of irrelevant. One of our agency's core values is that "every relationship starts with a click." It doesn't start with an open, and we're not in the business of "head-faking" someone to open our emails (except for re-engagement, perhaps) without achieving a click.

For this reason, the open rate is a dying metric to measure, and it certainly took a hit with iOS 15 rolled out. Even our subject line testing measured results on click rate or click-to-open rate because the ROI of opens were hard to measure.

**OPEN RATE BY DEVICE**

On a macro level, however, open rates can teach us some things about our email strategy, such as:

- Which subject lines work best for your subscribers or customers?
- Which emotions invoke a higher open rate?
- Which days are the best in terms of open rates?
- Which segments open but don't click?

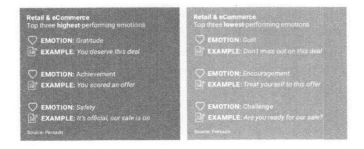

I love using Persado, an artificial intelligence subject line tool that uses machine learning to create emotional subject lines for every campaign.

Our team tested gratitude-based subject lines on post-purchase flows and achievement subject lines for loyalty and rewards campaigns. As you can see below, I did a case study with Persado because it was a really interesting and effective use of AI in our email & SMS program.

Subject lines offer a great way to mix copy with your creatives and reward the open with a click. For e-commerce businesses, the average open rate of a promotional email campaign is 18.3%, but once again, segmentation and personalization will increase that number significantly.

***

In this chapter, we've created a checklist of sorts containing the essential elements of a successful email, SMS and CRM strategy. With a cutting-edge ESP, ongoing flow of clean, actionable data, and measurable KPIs, you should now be fully prepared to implement a truly customer-centric email, SMS and CRM strategy.

The moment has finally arrived. Let's dive into the only strategy you'll ever need to create a more profitable, predictable, and sustainable revenue stream from email and SMS.

**Email & SMS Foundation Checklist**

Trust me. You don't want to miss a step when building your email & SMS foundation. When I onboarded new ESPs, technologies and vendors, a checklist helped keep all the moving parts organized and manageable. Now, I'm gifting this checklist to you! Our one-page Email & SMS Foundational Checklist will ensure you never miss a step and launch an email & SMS program as fast as possible. You can download this checklist by visiting HiFlyerDigital.com/foundation-checklist

# CHAPTER SIX

## The S.P.A.M. Strategy

We've finally arrived at the core strategy that's helped thousands of e-commerce brands like yours build better customer relationships and create profitable, predictable, and sustainable revenue streams.

The build-up is just as important as the strategy. None of what I'm about to share with you works without:

1. Understanding why you must compete with Amazon, D2C brands, and Silicon Valley if you want to survive and keep customers loyal, as I've clarified in chapter two
2. Admitting that most brands, perhaps even yours, have failed at email, SMS and CRM in the past and could be doing it a lot better for the sake of the customer, as explained in chapter three.
3. Underlining the urgency to act now - COVID-19 will most likely not happen again in our lifetimes - as shown in chapter four.
4. Committing to investing in an infrastructure that sets you up to succeed, as summarized in chapter five.

Let's start diving into the core email, SMS and CRM strategy that will help you build better customer relationships and help you create profitable, predictable, and sustainable revenue streams for your business.

**The Background**

I want to remind you about where e-commerce comes from. If you look up the definition of e-commerce, it is defined as "commercial transactions conducted electronically on the internet."

But I want you to think deeper as to what e-commerce really means for you as a consumer. Essentially, e-commerce is the art of replicating the in-store experience online. Think about it: e-commerce is supposedly the "death" of brick-and-mortar stores. Amazon and Walmart killed the neighborhood general store. Macy's and Sears greatly reduced their physical locations over the past decade due to e-commerce. Even today, malls are still shuttering their doors due to online shopping trends.

For consumers, e-commerce is a more convenient way to shop, yet they still crave a personalized in-store experience. Although, at a glance, these seem like polar opposites, I learned a lot by exploring the stores at the e-commerce brands I worked, consulted, and advised on.

This strategy I'm about to share takes into account that you are a consumer and that you buy stuff. Who doesn't, right? It goes further by saying that you, like most consumers, would like to be treated just as well digitally as you would be in-store, if not better.

I believe that if you excel in the in-store experience, you can excel in email, SMS and CRM. They're nearly identical in strategy and tactics, though entirely different mediums. If you want to connect with the person behind the email and SMS, you need to treat them as people. This strategy will do exactly that.

## The Four Pillars of the S.P.A.M. Strategy

Using the in-store analogy as a guide, let's dive into the four pillars of our unique strategy.

- SEGMENTATION

- PERSONALIZATION

- AUTOMATION

- MULTIPLICATION

1. **Segmentation** - finding the right person for your message
2. **Personalization** - personalizing the right message on a 1:1 level
3. **Automation** - automating the message to send at the right time
4. **Multiplication** - scaling automations up to run repeatedly on demand for multiple products, people, or goals.

Remember when I said I like to have things explained to me like a five-year-old? This is one of those times, and I like to break this down even simpler:

1. **Segmentation** – right person
2. **Personalization** – right message
3. **Automation** - right time
4. **Multiplication** – repeat

Right person. Right message. Right time. Repeat.

- RIGHT PERSON

- RIGHT MESSAGE

- RIGHT TIME

- REPEAT

**Right person. Right message. Right time. Repeat.**

We train our entire team on this philosophy and drill it into every client, brand, and vendor we work with. The essence of great email, SMS and CRM for e-commerce comes down to finding the right person, personalizing the right message to them, automating it to run at the right time for the customer, and repeating that process for multiple products, categories, and goals.

Keep saying it until it flows off the tongue: Right person. Right message. Right time. Repeat.

Obviously, by now, you've noticed another interesting mnemonic in our strategy – S, P, A, and M are highlighted in yellow. We call this our S.P.A.M. Strategy.

Now you're probably going to say that it's a terrible name and the play-on-words for SPAM is wrong and totally not what brands want to achieve. First, you'll quickly learn that this strategy achieves the exact opposite of traditional junk email; our clients have sent fewer emails and doubled their revenue, and it's all because of the strategy.

Second, you'll never forget a strategy entitled the S.P.A.M. Strategy, I guarantee you. And that's the most important part: remembering, internalizing, and sticking to the game plan.

Putting the plan name aside, the key phrase to remember is, once again, right person, right message, right time, and repeat. And the way to achieve that is through segmentation, personalization, automation, and multiplication.

I want to be very clear on the S.P.A.M. Strategy: you could excel in one or two of these pillars, but you can't scale until you excel in all four pillars.

I'll give an example: segmenting out shoe buyers and personalizing an email to them is a good start, but without automating the process, you're left doing manual work every time. You're also potentially missing the customer's shopping window because you're launching during work hours or sending campaigns instead of triggers.

You can't scale this either to other product lines or categories – like blue suits or dresses over $250 - because you may not have learned enough from the manual campaigns to create an automated process that works. Every pillar needs to reinforce the pillar before and after it to truly unlock the revenue potential.

Although you should take your time to ensure implementing all pillars successfully, don't settle for perfecting one or two pillars.

Winston Churchill said that "perfection is the enemy of progress." It's important to take an iterative approach here and try something out, learn from it, refine it and then move to the next pillar.

The goal of the S.P.A.M. Strategy is to personalize the customer experience for EVERY customer, automate the process for your team and scale up your email, SMS and CRM tactics as your business grows. You'll eventually hit a wall if you focus on only one or two pillars without putting the rest on your roadmap.

Now, let's dive into every pillar of the S.P.A.M. Strategy in-depth with a typical e-commerce use-case we can all relate to:

---

**S.P.A.M. Strategy | Use Case**

To bring the S.P.A.M. Strategy to life, let's create a use case to guide us. Picture this: you're a **men's fashion retailer**, and you're tasked with selling a warehouse full of **new brown Oxford shoes** priced at **$200**. You can even give a discount of **10% OFF** for the **next week**. We'll use this example throughout the chapter as well as zero in on the campaign components that are underlined above.

---

If you feel that this use case is unrelatable – though I'm confident we've all bought a pair of brown shoes at some point – then you can simply substitute your own brand and use case where I've underlined above.

Now, where do you start? Should we spray and pray? Should we blast the 20% OFF deal out there or try to keep our margins? Let's put the S.P.A.M. Strategy to work.

# Pillar #1: Segmentation

The first pillar in our S.P.A.M. Strategy is segmentation. We want to find the **right person** who would be interested in these brown shoes. I recommend you start creating high-level segments for this and then drill down deeper as you go along.

**Brown Monkstrap**        **Black Oxford**
**Shoe Buyers**        **Shoe Buyers**

Let's highlight some basic segments to start:

1. **Customers who bought black shoes**. People who bought black shoes would obviously be in the market for

brown shoes, wouldn't you say? It's a very simple segment to narrow in on automatically. You can swap out black shoes for brown shoes as well and see what that segment looks like.

2. **Customers who bought blue suits.** This goes a little deeper outside the shoes category. Pairing a blue suit with brown shoes is, to some, the height of fashion. Completing the look with a pair of brown shoes would make sense, agreed?

## Blue Suit Buyers pair well with Brown Shoes

3. **People who are browsing brown shoes.** This segment is more forward-looking. Instead of looking at historical purchasers of shoes, let's see who's in the market for shoes in the next few days. People who are currently looking at brown shoes online – no matter the style - are obviously in window-shopping or buying mode. They've shown high intent to purchase brown shoes quite soon. They would certainly pay attention to an email about those shoes, offer or not.

4. **Customers who bought brown monk strap shoes or brown loafers.** Like blue suit buyers, these customers

may be interested in completing their wardrobe with these complementary brown shoes.

5. **Customers who bought brown Oxford shoes over 180 days ago**. Do you see how every underlined portion of the use case is important in creating the segmentation? In this case, brown Oxford shoe buyers who bought half a year ago may be interested in the latest styles. This cohort bought the product previously and may love the new version.

**Brown Shoe Buyers over 180 Days...**          **...could use a new pair of Brown Oxfords**

These are just five segments to get you started on your segmentation journey. Over time, you'll get more creative and refined with these segments by measuring how each segment performs.

These segments aren't ranked in any specific order, so don't assume that black shoe buyers will outperform brown shoe browsers. Every segment should be built and isolated at the send level to measure incrementality. In my experience, however, I've seen that people in shopping mode outperform nearly all other segments, so you may want to consider that as the best segment.

It's important to remember that there will be crossover; for example, people who bought brown shoes obviously browsed brown shoes (how else would they be able to buy?), so be sure to suppress each segment from the one before it when launching a campaign to measure incrementality.

Any segments you would add here? Let's keep going down this rabbit hole with a few more advanced or "out-of-the-box" segments that could yield some opportunity:

1. **People who clicked an email in the last 30 days.** You may have found the perfect customer, but if they don't engage with email or SMS, they're not going to help move your brown shoes. It's important to layer in engagement into your segmentation; otherwise, you'll have a great on-paper segment that doesn't click.

2. **People who buy full-price shoes vs. discount shoe buyers.** Here's another great segment to help you determine who should get a deal and who can pay full price. Why give a deal to customers who are willing to pay full price?

Discount buyers &
deal hunters

Full price & high lifetime
value customers

3. **Shoe buyers who have a predicted lifetime value of $1,000+.** Finding customers who are projected to spend a lot of money with you - on socks, pants, shirts, and suits, perhaps - as well as bought shoes historically could help you capitalize on the true lifetime value of that customer.

4. **Customers who are about to churn.** This is a deeper strategy, but, in this case, a deal on brown shoes could be a good way to prevent churn. Weigh your current offers and determine if this brown shoe offer is good enough to prevent churn.

When applying to a real-life use case, be sure to outline the campaign theme and zero in on the key parts. In this case, the type of shoe, offer, timetable, and price point are leveraged when it comes to segmentation.

As you can imagine, we can go on and on with the number of potential segments. The point here is to zero in on the best segments, and you can only learn that over time. For example, if you only sent to shoe buyers, you could be leaving a huge amount of revenue on the table by not hitting shoe browsers or email clickers. The more segments you consistently identify and test out, the more your emails will resonate with that segment.

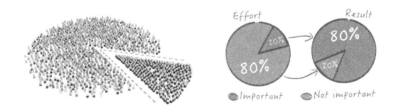

Historically, you may have identified a great number of segments in the past. Segmentation is probably the easiest pillar to conquer; you can probably visualize a whole bunch of fantastic personas, cohorts, and segments that would be a fit on paper.

I've faced many situations where brands think that their product will resonate with everyone and then fall back into a spray and pray perspective. Brands may go into a wishful thinking mode and assume that if we email everyone, the email may stir up some interest. I refer those clients back to the Pareto Principle.

Know this: the more segments you create, the longer it will take to execute. Try picking two or three incremental segments that you may never have tried and send them the campaign. Measure the results and try again. Keep iterating on new segments instead of just sending dozens of segments all at once. Break it down into manageable chunks for your team to execute.

Congrats! You've now identified the right people for this message. Now, it's time to personalize the message to the segment.

## Pillar #2: Personalization

Personalization is where most brands fail. This isn't an opinion. Go back to the McKinsey study, only 15% of brands actually excel at personalization, yet 84% of customers demand it.

While personalization is a top priority, only 15% of retailers have fully implemented personalization across all channels.

Finding the right segment is half the battle; personalizing the message to that segment is more difficult. The last thing we want to do is create a one-size-fits-all approach for every segment; that defeats the purpose of segmenting them out.

Let's go back to the store analogy. Imagine you're browsing blue suits. The salesperson - which is your email in digital terms — comes over and talks about the new brown shoes on discount.

You get kind of surprised and maybe even annoyed because you're interested in blue suits right now. It's kind of odd to request that I start pivoting to brown shoes right now.

The same applies here. If you have a segment who has bought a blue suit from you, you need to personalize the message to that blue suit buyer and talk about why these shoes are perfect for your blue suit. That's personalization.

There are a few key email and SMS elements that can be personalized:

1. **Send time**
2. **Subject lines**
3. **Preview/preheader texts**
4. **Copy & content**
5. **Design & creatives**
6. **Product assortment (dynamic recommendations)**
7. **Linking strategy**
8. **Landing pages**

Each element improves your email and SMS engagement rate in their own way; send time improves chances of open while product assortment increases chances of click, and so on. With so many elements to consider, you'll need to have a clear personalization playbook to keep you organized. Our C-4 Design Playbook is a great start, but use a checklist to ensure you're personalizing the message as much as possible.

Let's pull out a few segments above and show how we can personalize the email to the user.

# Blue Suit Buyers pair well with Brown Shoes

1. **Segment: Customers who bought blue suits.**
   a. **Personalization:** Using the C-4 Design Playbook, the email context can be geared around "completing the look with these brown shoes." Copy and creatives should showcase a blue suit buyer with these shoes and the OUTCOME they achieve with these shoes. If this blue suit is best for work, you can say something like, "Complete your work look with 10% OFF our new brown shoes, guaranteed to help you feel stylish in and out of the office."
   b. **Linking Strategy:** Go back to the intended destination. If you're promoting a product, link back to the product detail page (PDP), not a category page (PCP) or a listing page (PLP). A customer shouldn't have to sift through pages to find what you're promoting. If you're promoting a category of brown shoes, go back to a listing page that may convert better than a category page. All these different links need to be tested, but the point is to direct a customer to the most relevant and highest converting destination after the click.

c.  **Recommendations:** Remember, the customer journey is not always linear. Promoting blue shoes doesn't mean your customers won't buy something else. If the main message doesn't resonate with them, dynamic product recommendations allow you to share other products without distracting from the main message. A couple recommendation options for this email would be 1) other brown shoe options or sizes that would resonate with this segment and 2) non-shoe picks for blue suits, such as ties, belts, shirts, and pocket squares. I've found that algorithmically powered recommendations outperform manually curated items, so leverage the algo. It also helps save you time and will enable you to scale faster (as you'll see from the next two pillars).

d.  **Subject lines & Pre-Header:** Personalization goes way beyond just using the first name in the subject line. Similar to above, capture your segment's attention by personalizing the message based on their demographics, details, or previous purchase. A few examples of high performing subject lines would be, "The perfect shoe for your blue suit" or "Your blue suit's favorite accessory is now on sale!" or "Blue suit + brown shoes = stylish!" or "Isaac, a deal exclusively for blue suit fans!"

Let's see this in action:

| YOU MAY ALSO LIKE | YOU MAY ALSO LIKE |
|---|---|

## BLUE SUIT BUYERS - A

- Subject line: "Just in: the perfect shoe for blue suit lovers!"
- Preheader: "Even better: special offer inside, just for you!"
- Link: straight to PDP
- Recommendations: other shoe sizes or blue suit accessories

## BLUE SUIT BUYERS - B

- Subject line: "Your blue suit's favorite accessory is now on sale!"
- Preheader: "Isaac, a deal exclusively for blue suit fans!"
- Link: straight to PDP
- Recommendations: other shoe sizes or blue suit accessories

These campaigns are a perfect example of segmentation and personalization working together. From the subject line straight through the landing page, blue suit buyers have a personalized 1:1 experience that significantly increases their chances of engaging and converting.

The framework is amazingly powerful yet quite simple. For creative teams and brands that want to amp up their design even more, there are certainly additional components you can add here, such as a video, product blog post, or hands-on review if applicable. Keep the framework simple and intact, though. The right person gets the right message personalized every time.

Now let's take another segment and see how the personalization is different for this segment.

**Personalization = "SALE on New Oxfords!"**

**Personalization = "New Oxfords Everyone ♥"**

2. **Segment: full-price shoe buyers vs. discount shoe buyers.**
   a. **Personalization**: Using the C-4 Design Playbook, the email context can be split in two ways – deal-oriented vs. full price – opening a new world of possibilities. The context can now be geared around "First Look at our Newest Oxfords!" for full-price buyers and "Save on our New Oxfords Before Everyone Else!" for discount buyers. Subject line, copy, and

creatives should showcase the features, benefits, and outcomes of the shoes as it relates to each buyer persona.

> i. **For full-price buyers**: you can say something like, "First look at the perfect shoe for your work/life balance. With workday comfort for your 9 to 5 and after-hours style for your 5 to 9, check out our most in-demand shoe of the year." The creatives can feature the new shoe at its finest (GIFs tend to do this really well).
>
> ii. **For discount buyers:** you can pivot towards deal-oriented copy such as "Get early access + 10% OFF our most in-demand Oxfords, the stylish shoe equipped for work, home, and any time in between." The creatives here could focus on the shoe with a prominently placed button or ribbon indicating the offer of 10% OFF.

b. **Linking Strategy:** Once again, the link should direct to the best converting destination, which is usually the PDP. If you're able to highlight the offer on one PDP vs. another PDP, that would definitely help you keep margins on the full-price buyers.

c. **Recommendations:** Both recommendations algos mentioned above are still relevant here, but you may want to differentiate the items featured, prioritizing new items for the full-price buyers and deals for the deal-hunters.

d. **Subject lines & Pre-Header:** This is a great opportunity to split your subject lines. A couple high-performing subject lines for full-price buyers would be "New Arrival: The Perfect

Oxford Shoe" or "First Look at our Most-Requested Oxford." For deal-hunters, the subject lines would be more focused on the offer, such as "Our New Oxford's Best Feature: 10% OFF!" or "Our Newest Oxfords: Can We Deal You In?"

Sidebar: do you see how personalization is the most critical part of your email and SMS marketing? There are dozens of segmentation and personalization combinations that you can explore and discount vs. full price is just one of those combinations that you may not have considered. Take the time to think about what segments can be super personalized and invest some time in making it happen.

**Right person. Right message. Right time. Repeat.** Even just excelling in segmentation and personalization - the right person and right message pillars - will lift your bottom line significantly.

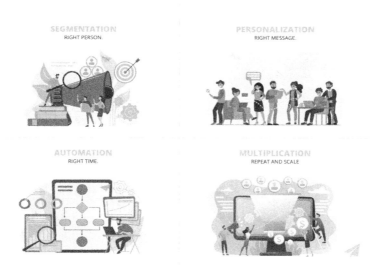

Ok, now back to our campaign design. Let's take a look:

## THESE ARE NEW FOR YOU!

## DEALS YOU MAY LOVE!

## FULL PRICE BUYERS

- SL: "New Arrival: The Perfect Oxford Shoe!"
- Preheader: "First Look at our Most-Requested Oxford"
- Links: straight to PDP
- Recommendations: other full price shoes, size & items

## DISCOUNT BUYERS

- SL: "Our Newest Oxford's Best Feature: 10% OFF"
- Preheader: "Our newest Oxford:DEAL you in?"
- Links: straight to PDP
- Recommendations: deals on related items, shoes & sizes

Both of these campaigns will perform extremely well in the KPIs you've set out - opens, clicks, conversions, and so on - because the segmentation and personalization are in sync.

Now, let's get real. Designing multiple creatives, creating persuasive context and copy, setting your recommendation algos, and ensuring a high-converting linking strategy can be a long, hard, and tedious task. Design can often be a bottleneck, so it can be very tempting to simply "get the email out" and sell shoes.

On top of the design challenges, you need someone to launch all these different segments and measure the results as well. **For these reasons, most brands fail at personalization, and if you fail here, you can't automate nor multiply your program to the next level.**

Don't give in. For brands that invest the time in great personalization, the benefits to your time and bottom line are monumental. A lot of heavy lifting at the beginning on setting up the right design playbook and processes will eventually get easier and smoother. There are a lot of creative tools on the market – Canva, Jasper, KickDynamic, and Persado, to name a few – that can help you get the ball rolling creatively and save you time.

I can guarantee you that if you take the time to perfect your segmentation and personalization correctly, you will see a huge difference in your engagement and conversions.

To quickly illustrate the power of segmentation and personalization within the S.P.A.M Strategy framework, I'm going to share a sample campaign that will show you how successful you can be with just the first two pillars of "right person" and "right message."

**Sent to 617k (50% less)**
**Earned $109K revenue**

**Sent to 288k (50% less)**
**Earned $190K revenue (70% more)**

See the snapshot above. Historically, this brand ran an evergreen postcard that said VIP One Day Sale with 40% OFF, and it performed well: $110K on average for a mailbase of 617,000. Not a bad day's work.

Enter the S.P.A.M. Strategy, specifically segmentation and personalization. Here's what I did:

- **STEP ONE:** I first separated the core segments driving the majority of revenue overall; in this case, our 2x Buyers + Canon, Nikon, Sony, and Apple brand buyers were the biggest revenue drivers, so we mailed each cohort separately.
- **STEP TWO:** I found every subscriber who browsed an item in the last 14 days - which indicated a high intent to

purchase - and mailed them a dynamic creative as well that resonated with them. This is a more advanced approach but highly lucrative if you can create it. I'll go into this in more depth in chapter seven, but here's the gist. If someone was browsing lenses, we'd say VIP One Day Sale on Lenses, or if someone was browsing tablets, we'd say VIP One Day Sale on Tablets, each version linking back to deals on those categories dynamically.

- **STEP THREE:** I shared my C-4 Design Playbook plan with my design and merchandising team, creating a one-click VIP creative that highlighted the offer and made customers feel like a VIP with exclusive early access, an emotional benefit. I requested up to six creatives instead of the usual one or two so each cohort sees something uniquely relevant to them.
- **STEP FOUR:** Our mailbase was 50% smaller than usual, but because of the Pareto Principle, I was positive we'd hit our revenue goals anyway. After being sure we were clearly tracking our KPIs of opens, clicks, conversions, and unsubscribes (as well as a few other advanced KPIs), we rolled the campaign out, starting with the browsed segment. Crossing fingers!
- **RESULTS:** The campaign was sent to 50% fewer recipients and made 70% more revenue, all due to personalization and segmentation.

Let that sink in. **This brand made more money by emailing fewer subscribers.** Isn't that fascinating? Not only did they extract more dollars from their email list and reduce the unsubscribe rate due to better personalization, they now focused their efforts on a more highly engaged, high converting segment.

In addition, the brand freed up 300,000 subscribers from getting a non-personalized email and had the opportunity to try something else with those subscribers or give their inbox the day off!

**Everyone wins with this approach.** The best segments feel more personalized, buy more and unsubscribe less; that's your 80/20 segment. The not-as-good segments could be sent an A/B test to try and get them to engage and become part of that 80/20 segment through a click.

With this approach, you'll hit your revenue goals with that 80/20 segment AND become a better marketer by testing out new ideas, strategies, and concepts on the not-as-good segments. Everyone - the brand, the customer, and the marketer - wins.

Personalization and segmentation always go hand-in-hand. When you perfect that blend, you will outperform all of your competitors. Remember, 84% of customers demand personalization, but only 15% of brands excel in it. Excelling in the segmentation and personalization pillars gets you into the 15% crowd easily.

But being in the top 15% isn't enough; I want you to aim even higher! I want you to get to the level of the top 1%.

In order to approach the top 1%, you need to be able to automatically create segmentation and personalization 24/7/365, breaking free from day-to-day manual efforts and creating personalized campaigns on auto-pilot. You'll need to conquer the next pillar: automation.

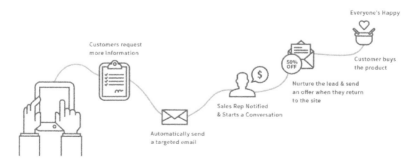

# Pillar #3: Automation

You've learned how to find the right segments for your campaigns and perfected the right message for every single subscriber in that audience. Now, using marketing automation, you need to focus on 1) setting your ESP to segment and personalize all day and every day and 2) send the right person the right message at the right time.

Let's be clear: sending at the right time doesn't just mean sending at certain AM or PM hours. It could mean one of the following:

- **Right time in their site visit** - when a subscriber shows an indication to buy - such as browsing, carting, or viewing an item - that's the right time to message them.
- **Right time in their purchasing pattern** - understanding when a subscriber is projected or predicted to buy is another right time to message them. This is equally important for replenishment items that are bought on a predictable cadence, as well as for loyalty and credit segments. On the flip side, if a customer purchased recently, it will be equally important to know the right time when NOT to send a promotional email, such as when a customer is waiting for their first order to arrive and not remotely interested in an upsell just yet.
- **Right time of day** - Time of day and site visit certainly need to work together, especially if you serve the entire U.S. market or even internationally.
- **Right time also means right channel** - it's not enough to simply send emails or SMS; you need to evaluate which channel is the best for the segment. Sending a cart abandon email to a customer who doesn't check their

emails is a missed opportunity; an SMS cart abandon may resonate better with this customer.

As you can see, automation goes beyond just saving your time. It's also about saving your customers' time and helping them get across the finish line conveniently.

To illustrate how automating your segmentation, personalization, and execution works, let's go back to our use case of brown Oxford shoes.

**Blue Suit Buyers pair well with Brown Shoes**

We've identified our segment - blue suit buyers - and we've personalized our email from top to bottom to resonate with them with one goal: get the click, which will lead to a conversion.

If you excelled in segmentation and personalization, your campaign managers are firing on all cylinders. They'd literally have a full plate of campaigns that can be super-segmented and super-personalized.

Their 9 to 5 would be completely full, and your designers will have lots of customer-centric work ahead of them. That means a high-performing email and SMS program... and a lot of burnt-out team members.

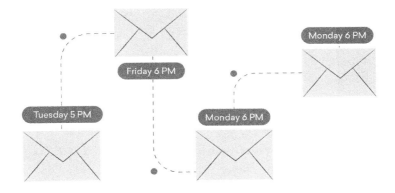

**Work smart, not hard.** If you have taken the time to perfect the first two pillars, focus all your efforts on automating that process going forward. If you don't, your team members will burn out and have little time left to analyze results, tweak strategies and iterate further.

Segmentation and personalization allows you to perfect the best experience for your customers. Once you know what works best, that's when you start automating the process to scale up for you. There are only so many segments, creatives, and campaigns that can be created in a day. Automation sets you up to scale 24/7/365 with little manual effort going forward.

Let's go back to our brown Oxford shoes example and break it down clearly:

- **Segmentation:** blue suit buyers
- **Personalization (using the C-4 Design Playbook):**
    - **Context:** the WHY is "Complete the Look"
    - **Creatives:** designed to show the context - blue suit paired with brown Oxford shoes
    - **Click:** click options include shoes + recommended sizes + additional accessory recommendations + a style video about the shoes
    - **Conversion:** traffic lands directly on the PDP

- **Automation:** when will this email be sent to the targeted segment.

At this point, running a one-off campaign is totally reasonable; you have the right segment and the right personalization, so a campaign would drive some pretty good revenue. Go ahead and fire it off.

But you don't want to settle for just a one-off send. You want to reach every blue suit buyer in perpetuity, every hour, day, and week that you can. Not doing so is a missed opportunity for you AND for the customer.

On the flip side, you also don't want to jump the gun and send the campaign too early or too late for the prospect to act. Imagine sending a brown Oxford shoes campaign to blue suit buyers two days after they bought the suit; they're still waiting for their delivery to arrive, and now you're trying to sell them more?! Imagine sending that campaign to blue suit buyers from three years ago; you're kind of late to the party, dude!

The solution is in automation. Using the blue suit buyer segment, you have to train your ESP to do the following:

1. Automatically identify a blue suit buyer at the moment of purchase
2. Set a predetermined wait period of X number of hours, days, or weeks - which is determined by either looking into your data for purchasing patterns or, let's be honest, sometimes a gut feeling!
3. Create your dynamically personalized campaign with PROVEN context, creative, and click points accurately.
4. Trigger your super personalized brown Oxfords shoe promotion at the perfect buying mode moment.

Here's the visualization of this:

**BLUE SUIT BUYER BROWN SHOE UPSELL**

**Wait Period**
Wait 30 days after purchase before upselling

**Launch**
Take personalized creative for blue suit buyers and launch at 9am (personalized send time)

**01.** **02.** **03.** **04.** **05.**

**Identify**
all blue suit buyers at time of purchase

**Decide**
Did the blue suit buyer purchase shoes during those 30 days?
- If yes, end automation
- If no, continue.

**Repeat**
Wait three more days, check if customer converted.
- If converted, end automation
- If not, resend with new subject line and offer.

**This is the power of email & SMS automation.** You can reduce nearly every manual function of campaign creation ONCE YOU'VE PERFECTED IT. I put that line in caps because it's important to know that "set it and forget it" isn't the end game.

You still need a marketing expert or strategist who can analyze the data, extract takeaways and set up additional testing where needed. Test, learn, refine; that's how to continuously perfect your automations.

Using automation, the only manual work you'll need to do is moderate your tests, learn from the results and refine them based on your learnings.

Let's take another example using people who've browsed brown shoes:

**BROWSED BROWN SHOES WORKFLOW**

Wait 24 hours after browse before decide period

Take personalized creative for brown shoes and launch immediately

Wait Period

Launch

01.
02.
03.
04.
05.

Identify

a user who has browsed brown shoes or shoe category

Decide

Did the shoe browsers make a purchase and / or cart an item?
- If yes, end automation
- If no, continue.

Repeat

Wait 48 hours and check if customer converted or carted.
- If converted, end automation.
- If carted, begin Cart Abandon
- If none, resend email with new subject line and offer.
- If email not opened, send SMS

Let me share an example of the automation pillar in action from my own experience. I once set up a first-time camera buyer automation with about twenty campaigns over the course of thirty days. Really advanced stuff; each email was based on where they clicked from the first email, sort of like a "build your own journey" book if you remember those!

As such, every email creative had multiple click-points within and was a creative masterpiece from our design team. There was a post-purchase thank you, content pieces, video links, accessories, links to sister brands, and so on.

After agonizing over every campaign touchpoint, testing the flow, and finally turning it on, we let it run for a month. I kept peeking in every couple days to see what was happening, as I tend to geek out over the minor details of automations.

After two weeks, I decided to do a "halftime report" on the first-time buyer series. I quickly saw some major takeaways; after the first two emails, our click rates declined heavily, going from 12% click rates to 2% between emails two and three.

Emails three and four went from 2% to .8%, respectively. What was the deal?

I realized very quickly that emails three and four were lens upsells. We figured that if you bought a camera, you would want to get a lens. Makes perfect sense at face value.

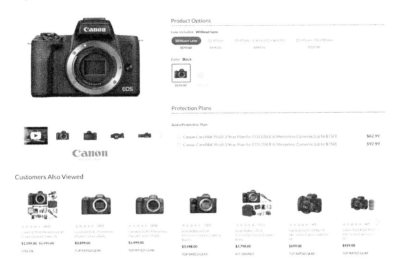

What we didn't realize, though, was that most of the cameras that were bought were camera bundles, and they came with multiple lenses. Our company had shifted to selling more bundles - to increase AOV and provide a unique advantage over Amazon - and consumers didn't need lenses because they had them in the bundle already. Hence, clicks declined for the lens emails for lenses they already owned or passed on.

I pivoted. I first decided to split out our camera buyers into three segments: camera bundle buyers, camera non-bundle buyers, and camera body-only buyers. Camera non-bundle buyers went down the same path as before since they were the target consumers the first-time buyer series was built for. The camera bundle buyers had a recreated experience that helped them learn what they can accomplish with their vast assortment of lenses and cross-selling them bundle accessories they wouldn't have gotten on their first purchases - such as bags, lighting equipment, and tripods.

The body-only camera buyers went on a slightly different journey. At first glance, I thought that they would be PERFECT for lenses; they didn't buy a lens, after all, only the body! After all, you can't shoot a picture without a lens. Wrong.

After looking at the historical purchases of some of these customers, I realized that body-only buyers were probably super-professional shooters who knew that they could keep their existing lenses and simply swap out their older camera body for a new one.

That was an AHA moment for me! And what did I do with that analysis? I positioned their email touches to focus more on trade-in your old gear offers - they have an old camera body to get rid of - as well as renting equipment for their weekend shoots and inviting them into our rewards programs, each of which was a highly profitable company offering.

The result was an improved customer experience, which was rewarded with 8% to 12% click rates… and a bonus at the end of the year for me.

Automation offers more than just removing manual labor; it opens up a world of possibilities through the data it unlocks. Sure, you can run a subject line A/B test on a one-off manual campaign to ten thousand subscribers. Trying to extrapolate learnings from campaign A for campaign B, however, is pointless; they're different campaigns, different times, and different variables.

Using automation, however, to run a subject line A/B test on thousands of subscribers with the same campaigns every day 24/7 will yield much more conclusive learnings. Automation allows you to run an entire testing schedule more efficiently, effectively, and confidently.

Going back to the blue suit buyer example, we can now identify what our automation will fill in for us:

- **Segmentation:** blue suit buyers
- **Personalization (using the C-4 Design Playbook):**
  - **Context:** the WHY is "Complete the Look"
  - **Creatives:** designed to show the context - blue suit paired with brown Oxford shoes
  - **Click:** click options include shoes + recommended sizes + additional accessory recommendations + a style video about the shoes
  - **Conversion:** traffic lands directly on the PDP
- **Automation:**
  - **Timing:** thirty days after purchase
  - **Testing:** subject line testing, run for 14 days
  - **Journey:**
    - End automation if item was bought
    - End automation if item was carted (cart abandon will kick in instead)
    - Resend email after two days if no purchase
    - Send SMS after three days if no purchase
    - Send profile to Facebook audience (for paid social efforts) after seven days if no purchase

Automation has filled all your gaps, and you can now run your campaign 24/7/365 confidently. Your time is freed up, your revenue is more predictable, your testing is automated, and you'll spend more time working on your business than working in your business.

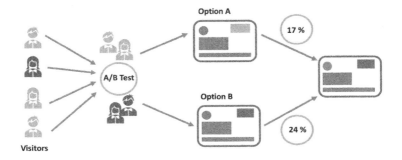

Note that there are important prerequisites you'll need to excel in some automations. First, you need to test what is the best predetermined time for these customers to buy again. Remember, a blue suit buyer may buy shoes one week later or maybe one month later. You need to constantly iterate timing to be sure you know the perfect time to launch.

Second, you need to consider if they're engaged with email or SMS. Too often, brands rely solely on email and SMS to drive sales without realizing that a consumer requires eight touchpoints before they buy - remember the customer journey? Be sure to consider other channels as well if your customers aren't as engaged after your first send.

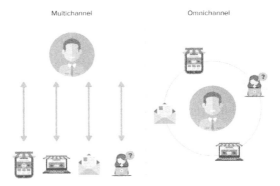

Third, you need to pay attention to the customer buying signals that are being sent to you every day. For example, if you've projected that a blue suit buyer is likely to buy brown shoes thirty days after their purchase, yet customer A has been engaging with your emails and browsing shoes after three days, that's a buying signal you need to act on.

This is where additional automations - such as a browse abandon - will pick up on the breadcrumbs left by your customers.

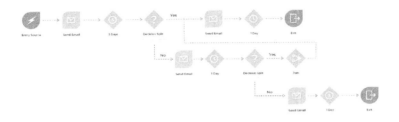

Fourth, it's never a one-and-done situation. Some brands prefer to run an automation like a campaign; one send, and you're done. Automation will let you create numerous touches on this journey towards your goal. For example, if a blue suit buyer doesn't open the brown shoes email, send their profile to SMS and send them a text with the same offer.

If the blue suit buyer clicked the email but didn't buy, automate a resend with a slightly different variation of your message; you're close to helping him complete the look, and they're engaged with email, so why waste that opportunity?

And if none of your email and SMS touches work, send their profiles automatically to Facebook and try spending some dollars on an upsell campaign. It's never one and done when it comes to automations.

Fifth, automation goes beyond just sending an email. You can set tagging automations that identify a prospect as a "VIP" or as a "Risk of Churn" or other tags, helping you segment out different types of subscribers.

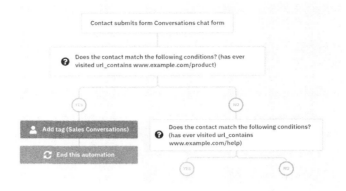

You can also automate suppressions, such as people who haven't opened an email in the last 365 days. Tag those people as dormant and remove them from your database, improving your deliverability. Automation will help you with every stage of the S.P.A.M. Strategy; it's a major revenue driver and time saver.

As you can see, if your automations are segmented and personalized, they will quickly yield the lion's share of your revenue. Your campaign and automation revenue percentages should, at a minimum, be split 50/50. Half the revenue from campaigns and half from automations, with the goal being even higher for automations over time.

However, campaigns and automations must go hand-in-hand. Think about it: if you don't send a New Arrivals campaign to your list, there won't be many people abandoning their cart to trigger a cart abandon automation. There won't be any browsing to trigger a browse abandon automation.

You need to fill your automations with clickers, browsers, and buyers; that's how the flywheel works. And automations will do the same: if a new customer clicks on a post-purchase accessories email, that will automatically trigger the browse abandon series, automatically placing them in a new buying journey that converts higher.

Eventually, your campaigns will just be basic emails that invite clicks. Ever noticed how some of the top brands send out a basic Deals of the Week or New Arrivals or Best-Sellers email that looks super generic?

Check out the very generic Best Buy emails I get every month; these are single click, simple contextual creatives that act as traffic generators for the hundreds of automations.

**FEBRUARY 2022**          **APRIL 2022**

**The reason for these generic campaigns is to get clicks, browsing, carting, and buying.** The automations handle everything else.

For example, if you click on video games in the 3-Day Sale, you can bet you'll get a series of video game campaigns automatically sent to your inbox, phone, and browser.

Here's another set of campaigns I get monthly from Wayfair, one of my favorite email and SMS brands. Honestly, do you think they really have Clearance every few weeks? These campaigns are traffic generators that get people into the funnel, letting automations convert them.

**MARCH 2022**    **APRIL 2022**

It's all designed in the same way - to get the click - and automated to run on schedule to get me to engage again. The automations do the rest.

Let's recap. You've learned how to find the right person (segmentation) and send them the right message (personalization). Now, you've also learned how to automate the process to segment and personalize at scale and send at the right time for the customer.

Now, with the final Multiplication pillar of the S.P.A.M. Strategy, I'll show you how to scale to different product lines, categories, and cohorts, turning your email and SMS program into a fully automated, segmented, and personalized revenue powerhouse for your business.

# Pillar #4: Multiplication

By now, if you have your email and SMS segmentation, personalization and automation dialed in, you're in a very good position.

You've officially eclipsed 90% of e-commerce brands out there and are entering the top 10% realm. Remember: our goals are to 1) help level the playing field and then 2) elevate you to compete and win at e-commerce. By now, you've certainly leveled the playing field.

The final stage in the S.P.A.M. Strategy is multiplication. You need to be able to multiply your segmentation, personalization, and automation efforts across multiple product lines, product categories, customer segments, and business goals.

You don't just want one brown Oxford shoe automation running to blue suit buyers; you want a black shoe automation running to gray suit buyers and a brown shoe offer running to brown belt buyers, and on and on.

You want to solve business goals like a win-back of blue suit buyers from over three years ago (churned buyers) and automate campaigns to blue suit buyers before they lapse (risk of churn).

Let's take a different product line. Perhaps you sell women's athletic gear and want to market a pair of women's running shoes. Since you've already done a trial run on the segmentation, personalization, and automation of a high-performing upsell campaign, all you need to do now is multiply the setup for these running shoes.

Everything is exactly the same. You can select one of the dozens of segments - let's take women's legging buyers - and personalize the creatives using our C-4 Design Playbook to connect with that runner on a 1:1 level - such as "go farther and faster with these running shoes that give back to the environment" or the like.

Segmentation =
Women's Legging Buyers

Personalization = "Get Fit
with These Running Shoes
You'll 🖤"

NEW
ARRIVAL

You're also ready to automate this campaign to every leggings buyer after 14 days without breaking a sweat.

You've officially achieved the Multiplication pillar. You've multiplied your brown shoe automation and turned the exact setup into a new women's running shoe automation that's segmented, personalized and automated.

Even better, within the exact same automation, you can have different paths and touches. For example, using a simple if/and statement, you can identify and split out two segments of buyers - like legging buyers and joggers buyers -and send them two separate campaigns.

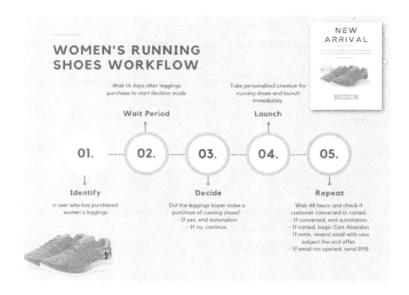

Here's an example:

- **Legging Buyers** - receive a "go further and faster" campaigns
- **Joggers Buyers** - receive a "the perfect shoe to go from runs to errands" campaigns

(Disclaimer: I haven't had the opportunity to buy women's apparel too often, so please note that this is just an example, not a styling recommendation!)

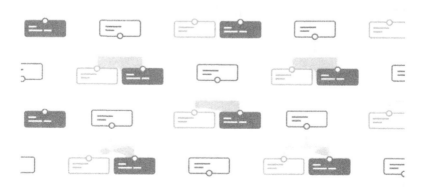

Through multiplication, you can layer in multiple segments, multiple categories, or multiple products into one automation or even multiple workflows. Your email and SMS program will be humming along really well and cover multiple goals all at once. That's what we call scaling. You've officially found a truly successful workflow that can be scaled over and over.

As mentioned, Multiplication is the easiest of the stages because the foundation stages - segmentation, personalization, and automation - will be perfected by the time you get here.

All that's left for you to consider is what possible applications exist for multiplying - or leveling up - your top automations. If your segmented and personalized automations work for brown shoes, it will most likely work for black shoes or blue suits. If your repeat-buyer automation works for moving one-time buyers to two-time buyers, it could probably work well for two-time to three-time buyers. Perfect the segmentation, personalization and automation and then ladder it up quickly using multiplication.

It's important to remember that you shouldn't try to replicate an automation that's underperforming or providing lackluster results; it's best to keep testing that automation to find a truly scalable workflow.

***

You've officially unlocked our S.P.A.M. Strategy, the unique email and SMS strategy of the top 1%. To create the perfect email and SMS program for your e-commerce business, you need to be an expert in segmentation, personalization, automation, and multiplication.

The only phrase you'll ever need to know is this: **right person, right message, right time, repeat.** At its core, the S.P.A.M. Strategy is super simple; you just need to segment out your audience, personalize that message to every user, automate the process to reach the person at their best time, and multiply those automations to scale your brand.

You saw what we did with one single campaign - 50% fewer recipients yet 70% more revenue - so imagine scaling that to 20 batch campaigns a month and 20 ongoing automations. Your revenue will increase drastically as customers spend more and unsubscribe less. The result: better customer relationships, increased loyalty, and unbreakable trust.

Yet each of these stages has a level of difficulty that will reveal itself. For example, if your data isn't clean, your segmentation could be off. If you haven't perfected the C-4 Design Playbook, you may miss the chance to maximize clicks and conversions and get frustrated with the results.

Automating this process will underperform, and scaling an underperformer leads to multiple underperformers. It's critical to take a step back and ensure the right foundation is in place - data, ESP, mailbase, KPIs, etc. - to excel in the S.P.A.M. Strategy.

But you're on your way! All the tools are at your fingertips, and you're set to start launching some really impactful campaigns and automations.

To get an idea of the type of performance you can expect from the S.P.A.M. Strategy, I've dedicated the next chapter to results and performance. There's nothing better than seeing great results and getting the encouragement to dive into a new strategy!

It doesn't matter if your brand is 10-figures or 6-figures; this strategy works for both big and small brands. In fact, the smaller the brand, the more nimble you can be with the foundational elements. Big brands benefit from having a lot more data at their fingertips.

The point is: everyone benefits from the S.P.A.M. Strategy.

And above all, the customer wins. Nothing is more important to the customer than knowing that they're being treated like a person, not an email. There's a person behind every email and text, and the S.P.A.M. Strategy is the best way to connect your brand with that person. The proof is in the data. Let's dive into the S.P.A.M. Strategy results.

**Free Video: The S.P.A.M. Strategy in Depth**

Studies show that reading a topic in print and then listening to an audio version will help you retain 10x more knowledge than by reading alone. So, I want to invite you to improve your content recall by watching our free 45-minute video on "The Complete E-commerce Email, SMS & CRM Strategy" (aka our S.P.A.M. Strategy) that I just shared with you. In this video, I'll vividly walk you through the exact strategy, results, and KPIs you'll need to implement this strategy successfully. In addition, I'll share a S.P.A.M. Strategy checklist so you can also stay on track with your four pillars. Reading, listening, and writing will increase your content recall significantly! You can start the video by visiting HiFlyerDigital.com/strategy.

# CHAPTER SEVEN

## The Results

Being in e-commerce, great marketing results usually come in the form of increased revenue. Whether presenting to C-level executives or small business owners, they all want that bottom line: did you make us money this month?

Usually, the answer is yes; we're very good at driving revenue from email & SMS. But over time, executives, leaders, and owners all start to realize that there's more at stake than just making money.

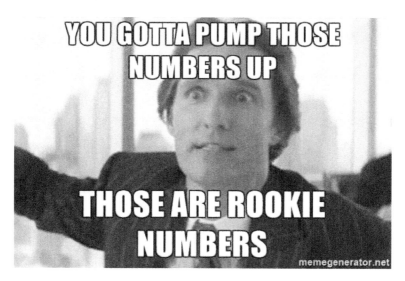

I'll give a good example of this. Back when I was just starting my journey, one of my old managers was able to drive revenue 30% higher in 2015… by sending 3x the number of emails! Our email footprint went from 5 emails weekly to nearly 15 emails weekly on occasion.

Imagine getting 15 promotional emails in a span of 7 days; you'd certainly unsubscribe and even report them to the FCC!

Over time, our list became exhausted, and although the revenue looked great, the number of churning customers became scary. As a result, the next year, revenue started dropping off. Having one great year at the expense of a lifetime of value was not a good trade-off.

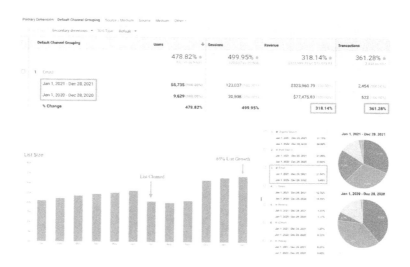

So, when I talk about results now, I always highlight more than just revenue numbers. I discuss correlative statistics and trends such as:

- Send volume vs. revenue
- Discount campaigns vs. full price campaigns
- Campaigns vs. automations ( % of total email revenue)
- % of revenue coming from email & SMS
- Customer migrations, such as 1x buyers to 2x buyers
- Order trends like AOV or conversion rate increase
- Incrementality of SMS, vendors, and tools
- Historical patterns and trends for the brand
- One-off anomalies (like a new item) that lifted revenue

- Trends in other channels that impact email (such as organic traffic decreases impacting email signups)

There are a lot of high-level strategic and analytical callouts that come with our email reports that I can pretty much deliver flawlessly by now in a deck, Zoom call, or in-person. And, of course, being that I like simple five-year-old explanations, my reporting is extremely clear and digestible.

So, the results I'm going to share with you go beyond the mere revenue increases our clients reap; the results are all focused around our core value: having a better relationship with every subscriber on your list.

## 70% Revenue Increase, 50% Fewer Sends

Let me start with one of my favorite ones; how the S.P.A.M. Strategy got buy-in from our entire executive and merchant teams. I shared this example briefly in chapter six - so some of this may sound redundant - but I'll go into a little more depth.

**Before the S.P.A.M. Strategy**

- Basic 40% OFF sale, one size fits all creative

**After the S.P.A.M. Strategy**

- Segmented emails
- Personalized to segment
- Automated data & sends
- Multiplied per category

See the snapshot above. The graphic on the left is a typical static one-off send that we all run - a 40% OFF Sale. The campaign performed relatively well, $110K on average for a mailbase of

617,000, and we ran it once a quarter or so. Not a bad day's work, but I felt we could always do better.

Enter the S.P.A.M. Strategy. First step, segmentation. I refocused the offer on our core brand buyer loyalists - Canon, Nikon, Sony, and Apple buyers - and set out to personalize their email experience from the subject line down to the URL.

In addition, instead of merely looking at historical data - such as purchases - we segmented out browsing segments to see what people were viewing now and potentially in the market to buy. Same goal; personalize their email experience dynamically at scale. Considering that this segment was roughly 30,000 people viewing a huge assortment of products and categories, I had to be able to personalize every single email with the category they were viewing. That was extremely challenging, but I was committed to aim high and iterate after.

The rest of the engaged population - such as 30-day clickers or openers - would simply get the regular version. I had to hedge my bets; after all, I had revenue numbers to hit, and I was uncertain about what the feedback would be from the execs!

The end result looked like this: differentiated creatives designed to resonate with each targeted segment. Sony buyers would get a Sony VIP One Day Sale and be linked back to Sony Deals on site. So would Canon, Nikon, and Apple. The destination would look like this:

The browsed version was very difficult. Not only did I have to DYNAMICALLY populate the subject line and creatives, but I also had to make sure the link went to the right spot and actually showed deals. Here's what I had to do (the brackets shown are the dynamic elements that needed to be populated):

**If a person browsed Lenses**

- Subject line: VIP One Day Sale on {{Lenses}}
- Preview text: Check out these {{Lenses}} TODAY!
- Creative: Grab these one-day VIP deals on {{Lenses}}!
- **... and link back to:**

brand.com/l/{{Lenses}}

**If a person browsed Tablets**

- Subject line: VIP One Day Sale on {{Tablets}}
- Preview text: Check out these {{Tablets}} TODAY!
- Creative: Grab these one-day VIP deals on {{Tablets}}!
- **... and link back to:**

brand.com/l/{{Tablets}}

Here's one the final outputs: I had to automate the data to incorporate browse data in the following places:

- Dynamic subject line
- Dynamic preview text
- Dynamic copy in creative
- Dynamic URL to land them

**Literally, the perfect challenge for the C-4 Design Playbook and the S.P.A.M. Strategy!**

Quite a lot of work, but the results spoke for themselves. After all the segments de-duped - there would obviously be a crossover between certain segments of buyers and browsers - I was left with just under 300K mailbase, half the typical volume for our campaigns.

Confident in my decision and empowered by the Pareto Principle, I pressed send. The results came through overwhelmingly in my favor. Our segmented + personalized approach made 70% more revenue while mailing 50% fewer people.

There's no better case study on the power of the S.P.A.M. Strategy than the campaign above. You may retort that this brand has a large mailbase and copious amounts of data, but I'll show you in the next few results that you have the same potential, same data, and same tools at your disposal.

You just need to have the right strategy in place, and that is the S.P.A.M. Strategy. This one campaign steered the strategy for the year, and all our mailings were styled in the same manner. As explained in a previous chapter, we mailed 40% fewer sends and grew revenue by 50% because of the S.P.A.M. Strategy.

## 4x Click Rates = 2x the Revenue

I won't go into a deep story behind this one because you've seen how the S.P.A.M. Strategy got fully adopted by one of my top brands. Let's just jump right into where they were and where I was able to take them.

This client's emails were great to look at, merchandised very well & highly aspirational, but the downside was:

- Batch and blast approach
- Little segmentation (local segments for stores mainly)
- Not much personalization
- No dynamic recs
- Links going to non-converting pages

As a result, they had:

- 12% average open rate
- 1.2% click rate
- 400+ avg clicks per send
- Subpar revenue and AOV, driven up mainly by the sheer send volume
- Conversion rate could improve

**Another great opportunity for the S.P.A.M. Strategy!**

Above is a rundown of this client's typical campaigns. This example illustrates that even the smaller brands can benefit from the S.P.A.M. Strategy. This outdoor cycling and apparel brand is one of the best in the industry at empowering its customers.

Where they saw challenges was in unlocking the true value of every customer, and they felt like they were leaving money on the table.

I opted to start with a basic New Arrivals email, which is always a good email to run as a test because it's so common, doesn't need discounts, and we can go wild with personalization.

**Using our C-4 Design Playbook, we created a New Arrivals email that:**

- Dynamic recommendations
- Clear context & relevant creatives
- Links to high converting pages
- Blend of product recs and manual merchandised picks
- Category navigation to invite exploration

As a result, they had:

- 43% average open rate
- 2.3% click rate
- 1800+ clicks (4x average)
- 2x revenue, driven by clicks, not volume
- 3x increase in CVR

Plus, bonus benefits as well:

- Cart and browse automations improved; more product views = more abandons triggered!
- Smaller segments = saving money on send volume.

**Another S.P.A.M. Strategy win!**

After segmenting out a bunch of new segments to determine which group of customers drove the most revenue - the 80/20 rule, remember! - I then set out to personalize the email for each segment. Loyal buyers got a different set of recommendations than the browse segment, non-buyers got a "wisdom of the crowd" set of recommendations, and the non-engaged segment got a subject line test.

Now, their calendar is peppered with multiple campaigns just like this one - New Arrivals, Best-Sellers, Top Deals, Expert Picks, and more - that will achieve their revenue goals in half the time and half the send volume. Another S.P.A.M. Strategy win.

## 2x Revenue Increase for a Billion Dollar Retailer

Just because a brand is one of the top retailers in the nation doesn't mean that they've tapped into the full potential of the customer base.

Once again, the S.P.A.M. Strategy works for brands of all sizes. Like I tell my clients - it's not about the list, it's about the relationship you have to the list, and I'm an expert at building better customer relationships.

Here's a screenshot of where this client started out:

As we've mentioned before, most brands should expect to earn 25% to 30% of e-commerce revenue from their email and SMS channel. As of March that year, this major retailer had email and SMS at 7% of total revenue and not even cracking 10%.

What caused them to start thinking differently? New management came in and wanted to refocus their energy away from merchandising and product-centric emails and more into customer-centrism and personalization. Definitely my cup of tea!

Without screenshotting their emails due to privacy, I took the same approaches I would do with every brand, and I highlighted the before and after below:

**Before the S.P.A.M. Strategy**

**Before the S.P.A.M. Strategy, one of our billion-dollar clients would run:**

- Batch and blast approach on 5M emails weekly
- No dynamic recommendations
- Heavy product driven emails with hundreds of items within
- Barely any segmentation (very surprising!)
- Preference center based personalization; if a customer opted into a Deal of the Day, that was the only email sent

As a result, they had:

- 15% average open rate
- .8% click rate
- Decent revenue, driven up mainly by the sheer send volume and high AOV
- Low conversion rate

**After the S.P.A.M. Strategy**

**Using our C-4 Design Playbook, we crafted a Newsletter that included:**

- Dynamic segments based on purchase history
- Curated products per segment
- Curated articles per segment
- Dynamic banners
- Personalized social feeds creatives with a clear CTA
- Dynamic subject lines, preview text, and context
- Category navigation to invite exploration

As a result, they unlocked a :

- 31% average open rate
- 4.5% click rate
- 6x the clicks to site
- 3x revenue, driven by clicks, and AOV
- 4x increase in conversion rate

Now, look at the revenue attributed to email as of October.

Their total attributed revenue jumped from $10M in March to $21M in October. Not only didn't the percentage from email nearly double, but it also translated into MORE than double the revenue from only months before... all with a few strategic tweaks from the S.P.A.M. Strategy.

Want another takeaway that would make the bosses and the bean counters happy? This brand can significantly reduce its ad spend now because email & SMS is doing better.

The brand can even invest in more opportunities for their stores, hire more staff, reward their marketing team with bonuses, test new technologies, and improve their customer experience... all due to the lift we provided them. These are the intangible benefits that come from implementing our S.P.A.M. Strategy.

FYI - the trend continued into November; they hit 14% of revenue just a few days later. Of course, the holiday shopping season hit then, so most brands see a lift, but because the email & SMS foundation was built, this billion-dollar retailer isn't going back to 7% of revenue ever again.

# From "Email's Dead" to "Email is My Best Performing Channel"

This is one of my favorite case studies, but not just because they're one of my favorite clients. This is one of my favorites because I helped shift an entire philosophy and mindset.

This client had a badly underperforming email channel; they were yielding maybe 1% to 2% of total revenue from email and spending a lot on paid search. They knew there was a better way to get customers to spend more, but they figured email was dead and didn't work.

I came in and brought my S.P.A.M. Strategy with me. By now, you've seen the C-4 Design Playbook screenshots and approaches I take, so I'll simply leave you with the end result.

This client went from 1% of revenue from email & SMS to 25% of revenue from email & SMS. Revenue increased by 530% year over year, and unsubscribes decreased. Why would anyone unsubscribe from personalized emails?

Talk about a mindshift: He personally said that my approach expanded his way of thinking about e-commerce - customer-centrism is the way to go! - and that shift has enabled him to scale up his business phenomenally over the years with no plans to slow down!

You can go to www.hiflyerdigital.com/case-study for the full case study video and hear it from him directly!

## Beating 12 Month Goals in Only 8 Months

I have many more examples of our S.P.A.M. Strategy in action - you can always email me directly at isaac@hiflyerdigital.com, and I'll be glad to send you our latest ones! - so, I'll leave you with these killer results.

Remember, the S.P.A.M. Strategy is more than just a campaign approach; the philosophy of "right person, right message, right time, repeat" should be rolled out to any email that goes out the door from your business. Automations, campaigns, workflows, nurture series, and even B2B emails should embrace the S.P.A.M. Strategy.

And here's what happens when you do exactly that:

## 2018 Full Year — Year Overview

| Year | Count | Delivered | Opens | Open/Deliv | Clicks | Click/Deliv | Click/Oper | Revenue | Orders | AOV | Conversi |
|------|-------|-----------|-------|------------|--------|-------------|------------|---------|--------|-----|----------|
| 2017 YTD | 494 | 291,482,983 | 58,601,384 | 20.10% | 5,209,065 | 1.79% | 8.89% | $47,344,404.35 | 87,896 | $538.64 | 1.69% |
| 2018 YTD | 425 | 257,375,931 | 48,233,811 | 18.74% | 5,533,095 | 2.15% | 11.47% | $72,918,300.86 | 124,247 | $586.88 | 2.25% |
| Difference | -13.97% | -11.70% | -17.69% | -6.78% | 6.22% | 20.30% | 29.05% | 54.02% | 41.36% | 8.96% | 33.08% |

**54% INCREASE IN REVENUE**
year-over-year

**41% GROWTH IN ORDERS**
year-over-year

**33% INCREASE IN CVR**
year-over-year

This client made 50% more revenue in 2018 vs. 2017… and mailed 12% less. We reduced our email footprint while hitting our goals early in the year.

For all those brands struggling with iOS 15 updates and how it affects email open rates, I'm kind of proud to share that we've always been ahead of the curve. Check this out; open rates declined by 18% but did it matter? Not at all. Relationships don't start with an open; relationships start with a click.

And the click-to-open rate jumped by 30%. That meant more visitors, more orders (41% increase), higher conversions (33% increase), and those game-changing revenue numbers you see. The kicker is this: I helped them beat their 12-month annual revenue goals in just 8 months. How would you like to have a 4-month vacation, knowing you hit your annual goals early?

The trend continued into 2019 and beyond - sending fewer emails and making more money due to clicks - all because the team embraced the S.P.A.M. Strategy for all their emails, not just campaigns.

## 2019 Q1 — Year Overview

| YTD | Revenue | GA Revenue | Delivered | Open/Deliv | Click/Deliv | Unsub/Deliv | eCPM | GA eCPM | AOV | GA AOV | Order/Clicks | GA Orders/Clicks |
|---|---|---|---|---|---|---|---|---|---|---|---|---|
| 2019 | $17,326,395.03 | $8,851,926.43 | 59,537,950 | 16.83% | 2.22% | 0.14% | $291.01 | $157.07 | $566.19 | $542.68 | 2.31% | 1.90% |
| 2018 | $12,983,993.27 | $7,286,784.14 | 66,785,168 | 20.62% | 2.07% | 0.17% | $194.41 | $109.11 | $519.63 | $501.98 | 1.81% | 1.05% |
| % Difference | 33.44% | 21.34% | -10.85% | 18.38% | 7.25% | -17.65% | 49.69% | 43.96% | 8.96% | 8.11% | 27.62% | 23.81% |

| MTD | Revenue | GA Revenue | Delivered | Open/Deliv | Click/Deliv | Unsub/Deliv | eCPM | GA eCPM | AOV | GA AOV | Order/Clicks | GA Orders/Clicks |
|---|---|---|---|---|---|---|---|---|---|---|---|---|
| 2019 | $6,064,080.15 | $3,188,194.91 | 22,927,307 | 14.11% | 1.96% | 0.14% | $264.49 | $139.06 | $616.96 | $578.62 | 2.10% | 1.23% |
| 2018 | $4,788,783.81 | $2,725,088.49 | 20,724,150 | 20.04% | 2.17% | 0.15% | $206.95 | $111.49 | $520.48 | $523.55 | 1.83% | 1.16% |
| % Difference | 41.39% | 16.99% | 10.63% | -29.58% | -9.68% | -6.67% | 27.80% | 5.76% | 18.54% | 10.52% | 19.67% | 6.03% |

**33% INCREASE IN REVENUE** year-to-date      **27% INCREASE IN CLICK/ORDERS** year-to-date      **10% DECREASE IN DELIVERED** year-to-date

Customers will continue to reward you when they feel you're building a relationship with them. Keep an eye on the engagement metrics that matter, like clicks, conversions, and AOV.

The S.P.A.M. Strategy works. Big, small, top 1%, bottom 1%; if you have a list of customers, start building the relationship that you and your customers deserve. Our proven framework is all you need.

# HOW JUDAICA PLACE
# GREW REVENUE BY 300%

**CLICK TO PLAY**

---

**Free Case Study Video: From "Email is Dead" to "Email is MyBest Channel!"**

Watch our complete case study on how I turned JudaicaPlace.com's email list into a profitable, predictable, and sustainable revenue stream, going from 1% of total revenue to 25% of revenue in just a few months. You'll hear directly from the owner on what his pain points and goals were, how I helped him achieve them, and where his business is today as a result. Find out why he now says, "if you've been burned before or had an agency experimenting with your money with nothing to show for it, trust Isaac!" You can watch the full 20-minute case study by visiting HiFlyerDigital.com/results.

# CHAPTER EIGHT

## Email + SMS: The Perfect Combo

I'm a big fan of text messaging. It could be because I'm a bit introverted, but I think texting is the BEST way to communicate your message in an easily digestible manner.

SMS is conversational commerce at its finest. You can simply dialogue with customers worldwide as if you were a friend. Your customer service team can simply text back answers to questions like "where's my order?" or "can I place a re-order?" Whole conversations can occur in SMS that aren't possible within the email channel.

If there's a person behind the email, there's certainly one behind the text. SMS connects with those people conversationally and promotionally.

On the promotional side of SMS, you can summarize a great campaign in just 140 characters or even with an MMS Gif. You don't need a full marketing team to design eye-catching creatives, QA your entire email, and then track a whole slew of metrics. SMS is easier to launch, has a quicker impact, higher engagement rates, and, well, is pretty fun!

**SMS**                                **MMS**

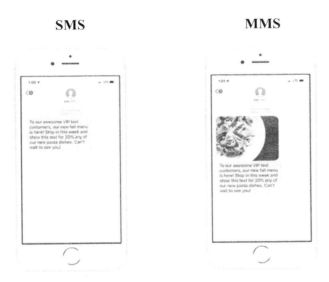

Just look at some of the great industry statistics about SMS for e-commerce that I compiled:

- 98% of text messages are read by the end of the day.
- 74% of consumers report having zero unread texts, and only 4% report having seven or more unread texts.
- 67% of people would rather text with a business about appointments and scheduling instead of communicating by email or phone call.
- 32% of consumers respond to promotional text messages from retailers.
- 48% of U.S. consumers prefer SMS loyalty communication over direct mail, email, or application loyalty communications.

- Nearly 35% of consumers prefer to receive coupons and promotional codes from retailers via text message.
- SMS engagement rates are six to eight times higher than email marketing engagement rates.
- 67% of consumers believe delivery updates are the most effective SMS messages, followed by order confirmations (64%), appointment reminders (64%), calendar reminders (54%), and promo coupons (49%).

All these statistics beg the question: will SMS replace email as the preferred method of customer communication?

Not a chance. There are a few reasons why email and SMS need to work in tandem.

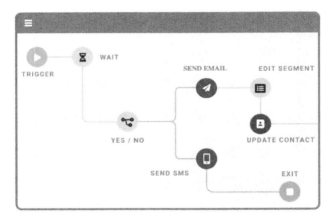

Remember that it takes at least eight touchpoints before a customer will make a purchase. Email and SMS are just a couple of those touchpoints. Of course, if you have the opportunity to market to customers via email or SMS instead of paying to reach people on search and social, you'll save money and keep more profits.

In addition, some customers prefer one channel over the other. I'm a fan of texts for quick alerts, but my wife prefers email. On the flip side, if I'm in shopping mode, I'm going to scan my email promotions to check for a sale or new arrival I'd like; it's not so easy to do that in a text. And with SMS, I'd only sign up for my favorite brands, not the most brands. With email, I can sign up and categorize those emails, so they're not clogging my primary inbox.

Long story short: everyone has a channel preference, so there's no chance SMS would replace email.

Finally, since SMS is a newer marketing channel, it's currently additive to email. If you decided to replace your cart abandon email with a cart abandon SMS, your revenue would take a nosedive. It's just not good business sense to remove one channel in favor of another.

SMS will allow you to communicate with customers who prefer SMS or simply don't engage with email. So, in the situation of a cart abandon, an email follow-up may be ignored, but an SMS cart abandon could be attention-grabbing.

Or, if you sent a Black Friday campaign on Friday at 9 AM and a reminder SMS at 3 PM, you could see a good incremental lift over simply sending another email.

Imagine all the situations where you can add SMS into an existing campaign or workflow. What you as a marketer need to do is measure the incrementality of having SMS vs. not having SMS. I can personally attest that when email and SMS work together, you'll see a strong incremental lift to your overall channel revenue and higher customer lifetime value.

Putting the attention, engagement rates and conversations aside for a second, there's a much deeper and more important reason to invest in an SMS program.

In 2023, Google Chrome will begin phasing out third-party tracking cookies, and brands need to be fully prepared to shift their marketing tracking abilities. Third-party cookies have long been a useful but imperfect method of advertising, remarketing, and identification, but with the rise of privacy concerns, Google Chrome is taking the lead on phasing those tracking cookies out.

## The future

Authenticated, durable IDs are used to connect first-party e-commerce customer data with second- and third-party data for efficient advertising, including prospecting and retargeting.

What does that mean for you? Ernst & Young took a deep dive into the future of cookieless marketing; their EY readiness model is above.

Ernst & Young declared that the best way to combat a cookieless future is by collecting as much first-party data as possible and capturing people-based durable identifiers. These first-party customer identifiers will keep you from experiencing any downsides on the marketing, revenue, and growth side.

Let's explain that to the five-year-old. Essentially, there are TWO main customer identifiers that are durable - meaning they are used across the web to ID a person - and you need to capture those identifiers before you miss the chance. What are those two identifiers? You guessed it: Email and mobile number.

I explained in chapter two that email and phone are unique identifiers, and with Google Chrome about to change the future of digital marketing, you need to collect as many opted-in emails and mobile phone numbers as you can. Build relationships with second-party data partners now, bolster your first-party data from existing customers and enable a better front-end method for customers to control how you use their data. All these tactics will help you get higher quality opt-ins and compete in the cookieless world.

Now that I've shown you the positives of SMS and the urgency of adding it to your first-party data opt-in strategy alongside email, let me show you how the S.P.A.M. Strategy will help you succeed in SMS as well.

## Step #1: Grow Your SMS List

You can easily grow your SMS list through pop-ups on your website, as well as text-a-keyword programs that can help grow a list on non-owned channels like social media.

Most brands nowadays do a two-step opt-in process where they request an email address and then sweeten the deal when you sign up for texts. This method is one of the best ways of building both lists, and you already have the subscriber's attention at that point.

Here's how to build your SMS list quickly with opted-in subscribers:

**Website Popup**

As shown above, the easiest way to build your list is with a website popup that sweetens the deal with an offer like a percentage discount. Most brands do a two-page opt-in where they request the email and then sweeten the deal further when opting for SMS. A/B test the experience to see what yields a higher submission rate.

### Signup at Checkout & Post-Purchase

There's no better time to gather as much data as you can at the moment of checkout. Request SMS signups right at the moment a customer places their order and adds their number to their account.

The most important part here is to manage expectations. Make these three things very clear:

1. Request that customers sign up for marketing updates.
2. Explain that they will be receiving text messages from you in a TCPA-compliant manner
3. Request that they provide their phone number in order to receive the text messages.

Here's an example of the copy that accompanies the opt-in (which is usually standardized depending on your SMS provider)

*I agree to receive recurring automated text messages at the phone number provided. Consent is not a condition to purchase. Msg & data rates may apply. View our Terms of Service for details.*

## Join our List Emails

No brainer. Send an email to your list, inviting them to join your SMS list. Use a one-click join link so they can sign up with little friction. Here are a couple of emails that do the job very well.

At the same time, don't just rely on a one-email approach. Put your signup link at the bottom of all your emails and highlight the numeric text-to-join keyword as well. You can also add this to the footer of every transactional email.

**Click-to-Text**

Texting a keyword to a certain number to join is a way to get offline signups into your SMS list. Events, in-store, packaging, and even social use click-to-text options for getting signups. This method of list building is simple and convenient and can be applied in numerous ways.

You can even change keywords to track different opt-in results. For example, your keyword EVENT can be for events, while LOCAL can be for in-store signups, giving you an additional data point for customer segmentation.

In addition, be sure to set your privacy and compliance foundation up correctly. Using Klaviyo, Postscript, Attentive, SMSBump, or another vendor, you generally have tools for creating:

1. TCPA-compliant language to update your Terms of Service & Privacy Policy.
2. Language to ensure you're receiving proper consent at checkout.
3. In-conversation opt-in confirmations and opt-out prompts.
4. Automated waking hours and overnight automation delays.

5. Double opt-in technology.
6. Automated opt-out and unsubscribe keywords (like STOP)
7. Pre-built, compliant popups and sign-up forms.

Set these up as you prefer. In my experience, these are time-consuming but will save you a lot of headaches and missed opportunities in the future!

## Step #2: Turn on SMS Triggers

Transactional SMS triggers are a great place to begin your SMS program. Getting texts with order updates, shipping confirmations, and account creations allows you to build a level of SMS trust and transparency.

Some of the high-engagement SMS triggers include:

- Order confirmation
- Shipping confirmation
- Payment updates
- Delivery fulfilled
- Updates and reminders
- Appointment confirmation
- Order replenishment

All of these triggers serve as traffic generators back to the right destination and should be highly dynamic. These kinds of messages are non-intrusive and incredibly relevant to customers. Plus, it reduces customer service inquiries, calls, and emails about order details or other needs, giving your CS team a well-deserved break.

Building your SMS program around transactional triggers will position you as a genuine source of help and education. Think of how you would communicate with a friend if they got an order they were anxiously waiting for; you'd excitedly ask, "Hey, how was the delivery?" or "Need help setting it up?"

In the Post-Purchase Hourglass chapter, you'll learn that helping your customers adopt their product will help you go a long way toward building customer loyalty and lifetime value. Use SMS as a source to be conversational, helpful, and educational before promotional.

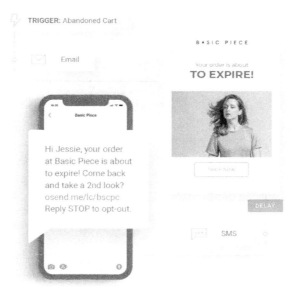

After you turn on the personalized transactional triggers, start building out the promotional triggers like welcome, cart abandon, and browse abandon.

You'll need to map out what the journey looks like so as not to conflict with email but rather reinforce the journey and delight the customer. Set the tone for what to expect via SMS in the same way you do for email.

## Step #3: Implement the S.P.A.M. Strategy

By now, you're already rolling out the S.P.A.M. Strategy for your email program (of course!), so take the time to level it up to your SMS program.

I won't go into every single stage again, but I'll highlight what each stage means to SMS. Since your strategic juices are flowing for email already, you've probably identified some great SMS applications as well, so let's see if we're on the same track!

### Segmentation

Finding the right SMS person can be duplicative or additive to your email program. Using our brown shoe use case again, identifying brown shoe buyers is pretty standard, but you'll want to segment out further by 1) email + SMS subscribers, 2) email only, and 3) SMS only.

The SMS-only segment is incremental to your email program and vice versa. The email and SMS segment is going to be quite valuable. If a customer wants to hear from you on BOTH channels, that's a potentially loyal customer!

Finding the right person for your message is as critical for SMS as it is for email. Zero in on the right population for your messages.

Set up SMS automations to gather first-party data that will help you fill any gaps. A survey does a wonderful job at providing actual user data from their responses; see the examples below.

Segmented texts and surveys do a great job at gaining ACTIONABLE data using numeric values, such as 1 for great experience, instead of vague responses like, "My experience was like me, fruity yet oddly appealing, thanks for asking!" These brands can now populate the next message - via SMS and email! - with a highly relevant follow-up based on the numeric value..

SMS allows for these types of conversations to occur, whereas email is a more direct response and promotional. Take advantage of the conversation to get the actionable data you need to segment better.

## Personalization

SMS personalization comes down to a really great context and how you get that across in 140 characters. Above 140 characters and you're faced with a two-text message (which could be annoying to some subscribers) and additional costs.

The key part is to be conversational while slightly promotional and invitational. A great one featured above is the CB2 text on the right that was sent on Thanksgiving Day, asking if you "need a chance to escape the in-laws" and directing subscribers back to their holiday sale. This is a great example of being conversational and promotional.

Some brands elect to send MMS and use GIFs or pictures to accompany the text; you should definitely measure the incrementality of animated images. CB2 again does a great job of creating a survey-type GIF for segmentation purposes and following it up with a personalized promotion.

CB2 speaks to their customers like a friend getting texts, and that's the magic of SMS personalization. In addition, CB2 makes sure to stagger their messaging, so an email and SMS don't come in at the same moment for subscribers opted in to both channels, improving engagement and ensuring incrementality.

**Automation**

We've already discussed that the core transactional and marketing triggers should be turned on, regardless of the strategy, so I want to primarily show you where SMS automation becomes a great contributor to your bottom line.

Let's take a cart abandon automation. Of course, you can have an SMS cart abandon text for people who are signed up.

Here's the tricky part: how do you best orchestrate email and SMS to work together to recoup the cart instead of poaching the sale from the other channel?

First pass goes to email; no surprise as that's the cheapest and highest ROI channel. Once I run a check against the engagement of the first email, I can run an additional check on if the customer is subscribed to SMS. If so, and the subscriber ignored my first email, I send an SMS cart abandon. On the flip side, if the customer is ONLY subscribed to SMS and not email, we send them an SMS first (this is a separate automation).

SMS needs to be able to fill in the gaps in your cart abandonment that may be overlooked. Above is a simplified example of a multi-channel cart abandon that some of the top brands run.

Using this logic, if the email was engaged with, send another email since the subscriber is responding to the channel and save SMS for later. After running another check after the second campaign, I can then opt to 1) send to customer service with a note to call them about their cart or 2) send them over to Facebook for a retargeting campaign and spend a few shekels, or 3) send a third cart abandon email or SMS with an offer this time and spend some more shekels. Note that this is the last option in this flow; why give a discount until you absolutely need to?

Creating a clear journey map using automation, you can orchestrate all your marketing channels to work together instead of in a silo. Each channel will be personalized to the subscriber and help contribute to closing the sale every time.

In the case of customer service calls, that's a business decision. Some retailers can actually offer a better discount by phone to close the deal than by email (MAP violations and all). Other brands have a really close connection to their customers and are comfortable calling them up; this is especially applicable with high item values where customers may need some hand-holding to complete the order.

The combinations, wait times, audiences, send time, and actions should all be mapped out and customized to your brand. You may prefer to send an SMS a couple hours after the email or opt to send the cart abandoners straight to Facebook or split VIP customers vs. non-customers. I've ran these all, and I can honestly say these are all business decisions for you to test, learn and iterate.

Overall, SMS can either play a primary or reinforcing role in marketing automation.

**Multiplication**

When it comes to SMS, as well as push notification, in-app notifications, retargeting, and browser push, the multiplication pillar needs to be interpreted as multi-channel. Considering you've turned on the core SMS triggers, focus this step on making SMS additive to all your automations.

Similar to how we mapped out for cart abandon, think about where SMS can play a role as an added channel for an existing automation. Here are a few examples:

- Rewards & Loyalty: receiving text alerts about a reward tier, earned reward, or expiring points is a great way of using SMS.
- Birthday Texts: getting a birthday email is nice, but most people are used to getting texts or social messages.
- Replenishment/Text-to-Order: simplify the re-order process by offering an easier "text-to-order" automation when the customer wants to replenish; customer service may need to handle this if you want to scale it.

Just like email, segmentation, personalization, and automation all apply to these SMS strategies. But because of the conversational tone of these texts, you may need a point person or agency to manage the inbound correspondence.

# Step #4: Launch Conversational Campaigns

Now that you've built your lists, turned on your core triggers, and implemented the S.P.A.M. Strategy into your SMS playbook, all that remains is pushing subscribers into the flywheel!

Important: the cadence of communication with your SMS list is very different than your email list. SMS is an extremely intimate channel and is a form of conversational commerce. Sending a text a day, like some brands do with email, is a non-starter so focus on quality over quantity.

It's perfectly reasonable to supplement your existing email campaign calendar with SMS but make it reasonable and segmented. Bear in mind as well that your SMS automations are part of that communication cadence, so be extremely focused with what you send.

Aside from the number of texts, focus on great copy and context. You only have a certain number of characters to start a conversation. Below are a couple SMS screenshots from my phone - one with a mass of promotions and then one on the right from North Face.

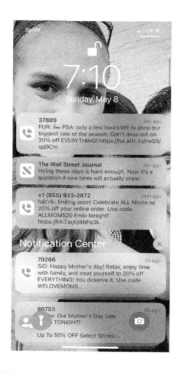
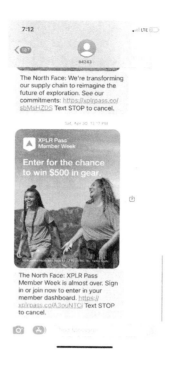

Although I'm sure that the texts on the left performed decently well, note how North Face intrigues me even more with a pseudo-loyalty offer, great MMS image, and clear call-to-action. Since I'm signed up for all these brands' email and SMS lists, I can say that North Face separated their messaging a day apart while the others blitzed me at once. It's clear that the other brands want to sell me, while North Face wants me to join their mission and community.

I personally ended up engaging with North Face and entering to win; the other brands didn't tell me anything different than the emails they sent on the same day. North Face reinforced their email with an SMS that took a more conversational approach.

The point is this: treating SMS like email is a surefire way to burn your list down. Texts should be conversational, personalized, friendlier, and to the point. This is where copy plays a critical role.

Consider using a tool like Jasper.ai or Persado to create a great copy with limited character counts. With a few simple tweaks to your tone, you can turn "last chance for your discount" into more playful copy and emojis without sacrificing bandwidth.

***

Let's summarize. I've shown you how easy it is to harmonize SMS with email using the exact same S.P.A.M. Strategy framework, providing an incremental revenue stream that is entirely customer-centric. Eventually, SMS will be a completely stand-alone channel for your business.

With the S.P.A.M. Strategy in place for your email and SMS programs, now's a great time to dive into our C-4 Design Playbook in more depth so you can excel at the hardest pillar of the S.P.A.M. Strategy: customer personalization.

**Free Guide: SMS Launchpad**

SMS is one of the most intimate methods of marketing, so you have to be sure to launch it the right way. Getting burned is NOT an option. In our SMS Launchpad guide, I'll highlight the best strategies for launching your first SMS campaign as well as share advanced techniques that will help you blend email and SMS together for maximum customer impact. You can download the full guide by visiting HiFlyerDigital.com/SMS.

# CHAPTER NINE

## C-4 Design Playbook

I remember sitting in meetings with our creative team and merchandising teams, hammering out a few new product announcements to our audience.

Our merchant teams were super-passionate about the new products; they could rattle off dozens of fantastic new specs, features, and attributes.

Our creative team was excited to be able to showcase all those features with some mind-blowing graphics, bullet points, and banners. Considering there were a few product variations, the email would be a work of art, designed for easy scrolling and maximum readability.

I could sense the passion in the room and stepped back to let the product and creative experts take the lead. Bear in mind I was only a few months into the role - I hadn't even created my S.P.A.M. Strategy yet - and figured I'd listen more, talk less and defer to the seasoned vets.

Creative without strategy is called 'art.' Creative with strategy is called 'advertising.'
Jef I. Richards

After the campaign was whiteboarded, tweaked, erased, and whiteboarded multiple times again, the merchants and designers agreed on the approach. Designs were mocked up, proofed out, and greenlit.

Results from the launch came in: 15% open rate, .5% click rate, and around $20K in sales from a half-million mailbase. Management had a hard time accepting those engagement metrics and sales numbers.

We came into a post-mortem meeting, and the accusations flew; the creatives were too long, the product specs weren't highlighted enough, the mailbase was too small, the product specs were highlighted too much, our competitors beat us to market, the price was too high, and so on. Fingers were pointed, and blame was distributed.

From then on, I took a more active role. After all, OUR TEAM was tasked with revenue goals; if the revenue wasn't growing, that would be a black eye on us. Luckily with email and SMS, the metrics for success are obvious - low clicks come from weak creatives, copy, and personalization - so I needed to be sure I could track every possible touchpoint that the customer experienced when I launched a campaign.

Those touchpoints included the copy, the creatives, and the landing pages, so I needed to be sure I could orchestrate all those teams under one unified creative strategy for the sake of the customer and the business.

Copywriters will tell you that copy is the most persuasive part of your marketing. UX will tell you that the landing page and customer experience is the most important part of the journey. And your creative team will be adamant about why the creative is key to every sale.

Having worked with dozens of teams, workers, and departments, as well as tested every possible variation of copy, content, creative, and conversion, I can confidently say that not one single creative option fully wins the customer over. This is why I created the C-4 Design Playbook.

Copywriters can persuade, but they may not get the click. Creatives may get the click but may not get people to convert. UX may get people to convert, but if the traffic isn't there, thanks to great ad copy and clicks, there's no scale.

Every element must work together to attract, engage and convert the customer. The C-4 Design Playbook puts all the control in the hands of the customer-centric strategist; if you put the ownership into any one of the creative teams, you'll get unduly influenced in one creative direction.

Jeff I. Richards, a professor at Indiana University, said, "Creative without strategy is called art; creative with strategy is called advertising." That line rings true for e-commerce marketing. With hundreds of creative tests under my belt, I've pieced together our C-4 Design Playbook to incorporate the top four strategic elements for great email and SMS marketing.

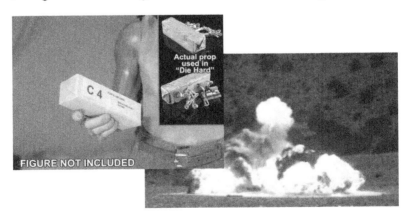

The C-4 Design Playbook comes from the old action films back in the day where the bad guy always seemed to get their hands on some C-4, a highly volatile plastic explosive. Bruce Willis or Arnold Schwarzenegger would always stop it from detonating, to the delight of moviegoers, but clearly, it was some highly explosive contraband.

Being a little cheesy, I decided to take our four-step creative process that would "explode" your sales and create another playful mnemonic for our clients to remember. Hence, the C-4 Design Playbook was created, and it's provided fantastic clarity, buy-in, and results from every business, team, and stakeholder we've met.

Let's jump right into the four C's of our C-4 Design Playbook: context, creatives, click, and convert.

## Stage #1: Context - Accentuating the Why

Remember in chapter one when I discussed Simon Sinek's *Start with Why: How Great Leaders Inspire Action* TED Talk? Accentuating why a subscriber should stop and pay attention to you and your message is the first step in the C-4 Design Playbook.

Let me summarize his TED Talk and tie it in to our C-4 Design Playbook. Using his golden circle visualization, Simon claims that most brands communicate from the outside in. for example, Dell makes great computers that are custom-made, easy to assemble, and affordable. Brands like Dell focus on WHAT they do and HOW they do it, never once reaching the WHY they do it and WHY it matters.

The great brands, however, like Apple, communicate from the inside out. For example, Apple markets itself by saying, "everything we do, we believe in challenging the status quo, we believe in thinking differently." And HOW do they do that? By creating products that are beautifully designed, easy to use, and user-friendly. Apple just happens to make computers.

Because Apple thinks differently, they attract people who think differently and want to change the status quo. And no matter WHAT they sell - computer, iPad, iPhone, Apple Watch - people will buy it because Apple's WHY matches their customers' WHY. Apple customers ALSO change the status quo, so they gravitate to everything Apple sells.

Simon also compares Apple to Dell; when Dell came out with an MP3 player, no one bought it. Why? Because to everyone, Dell is a computer company. Why would anyone buy an MP3 player from a computer company? Dell does computers. That's WHAT they do.

Yet Apple is also a computer company, and the iPod was their biggest seller for years. Why? Because Apple thinks differently. Apple led with their WHY, not their WHAT or HOW. And everyone that believes in what Apple believes will literally buy everything Apple sells, even when they go beyond computers. And true to form, everything Apple sells challenges the status quo every time, from phones to watches.

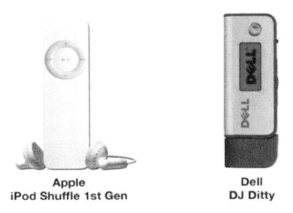

**Apple**
**iPod Shuffle 1st Gen**

**Dell**
**DJ Ditty**

**It's not about WHAT you do; it's about WHY you do it.** Tying this message into the C-4 Design Playbook, all your customer-centric marketing needs to focus on the WHY of your product, offer, and message, not the WHAT or the HOW.

So, how do you accentuate WHY this message, product, or offer is important? Through a consistent focus on features, benefits, and outcomes for the end-user.

Let me pause for a moment and mention that copywriting and content are important but not as a stand-alone entity.

Let's go back to the brown shoe use case. We had a good offer on brown Oxford shoes and could easily summarize the campaign context as "20% OFF Brown Oxford Shoes, Limited Time Only." And it would perform decently among people who are in the market for brown Oxford shoes.

But what about the 97% of people who aren't in buying mode. What's the true context that will get them to stand up, pay attention and convert at the same if not higher than the people in buying mode? Take a page out of Apple's marketing playbook; what's compelling their fans to stand in line for hours to get the latest iPhone or iPad?

That call-to-attention is what the context provides: features, benefits, and outcomes that the subscriber wants to truly achieve. Going back to the brown shoes, let's break it down further:

- Features: what does this shoe have that no other shoe before it contains?
- Benefits: what is the benefit for the end-user?
- Outcome: what will they achieve by using those shoes?

It's coming together now: these lightweight, flexible brown Oxford shoes are designed for work, home, and play, giving you comfort for your 9 to 5 and style for your 5 to 9. And it just happens to be 20% OFF.

- Features: lightweight, flexible, brown, Oxford
- Benefits: comfort and style for everywhere you go
- Outcome: you can achieve more when you work comfortably while still being stylish from work hours to after-hours

The sweetener is 20% OFF. You've now communicated from the inside out: you led with the outcome and benefits - the WHY - and stacked the features and offer on top of it - the HOW and WHAT.

Here's a great example from AllBirds.

Lightweight, breathable eucalyptus fiber provides next-level comfort

Cushioned midsole gives wear-all-day support

Machine-washable materials keep shoes looking like new

CASTOR BEAN INSOLE
**Plant Your Feet In Comfort**

We layered castor bean oil, which emits less carbon than petroleum-based foam, and ZQ Merino wool for a cushiony, moisture wicking, and odor reducing insole.

Because AllBirds has an audience that is 100% eco-conscious, they lead with their eco-friendly mission - the WHY they exist - and show what features lead to benefits for you. Lightweight, breathable eucalyptus fiber leads to next-level comfort, which means you'll achieve more while giving back to the planet.

Let's take another example using a computer. I have a lot of experience selling consumer electronics, and I'll be the first to tell you that computer specs simply don't sell the product. The key is to take those features and create outcomes for them.

A feature of a 10th Gen Intel Core i5 yada in yada - essentially, the WHAT - is not enough to get me to buy this computer. But the outcome of being able to work smarter and not harder - the WHY - is actually VERY compelling for an entrepreneur like me. See the screenshot below.

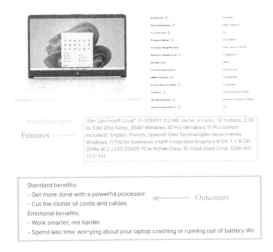

Features

10th Gen Intel® Core™ i5-10500T (12 MB cache, 6 cores, 12 threads, 2.30 to 3.80 GHz Turbo, 35W) Windows 10 Pro (Windows 11 Pro license included), English, French, Spanish (Dell Technologies recommends Windows 11 Pro for business) Intel® Integrated Graphics 8 GB, 1 × 8 GB, DDR4 M.2 2230 256GB PCIe NVMe Class 35 Solid State Drive 3280 AIO 21.5" FH

Standard benefits:
- Get more done with a powerful processor.
- Cut the clutter of cords and cables.
Emotional benefits:
- Work smarter, not harder.
- Spend less time worrying about your laptop crashing or running out of battery life

Outcomes

In fact, one of our agency's core values is to work smarter, not harder, so this laptop would greatly appeal to my inner WHY.

Boston Market turns ordering food into a need; at 10 AM on a wintery Saturday morning, I do need some comfort food right now, sure! The WHY is the comfort of home on a cold day, and the offer and free delivery is the proverbial cherry on top.

Turn your HOWs and WHATs - such as features, offers, and details - into a context of WHY and your message will resonate significantly better. The context should be displayed consistently on creatives, landing pages, and PDP, as you'll learn next.

## Stage #2: Creatives - Bringing Context to Life

The creatives are where your context comes alive. It's one thing to map out the message, tone, audience, features, benefits, and outcome in your creative briefs; it's an entirely different task to create the final design in an easily digestible, contextual, and direct response format.

Here are some great visuals that truly bring the context alive:

- Brooklinen: Their WHY is to be ridiculously comfortable, and that means having the ability to mix and match easily; they show that in the copy and animated GIF. They add on the HOW (neutral beauties) and the WHAT (new sheets / limited edition / scarcity).
- Casper: Their WHY is to help you get better sleep, and they show that with a great tagline (Come back to bed instead of come back to cart) and a review highlighting how customers get great sleep.

- Best Buy: In a few words, their WHY - make your home smarter - is portrayed in a middle-class home that could use an upgrade along with HOW and WHAT products that will get you there.

Best Buy's email below is a great example of creating a visualization for the campaign context. Their WHY in this campaign make outdoor living easy and fun; the HOW and the WHAT are smart tech, eco-friendly gear, and easy-to-use appliances.

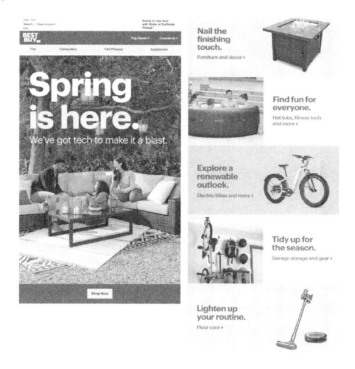

"Lighten up your routine" hits the customer with a couple emotional benefits: making cleaning easier on your time and body. The hands-free Roomba and lightweight Dyson achieve that exact outcome.

Let's take another one. "Nail the finishing touch" appeals to outdoor enthusiasts who love spending time outside. The fire pits and decor - the WHAT and HOW - are an extra bit of luxury that will "finish" that backyard and help "nail" that sense of DIY accomplishment.

These subtle context messages are super persuasive, and the visuals are clear and actionable. Best Buy's designers took a huge seasonal concept - Spring Tech & Home Electronics - and broke it down into contextual banners and blocks. There's no need for paragraphs of copy, FOMO messaging, or animated GIFs; the creatives summarized the WHY, HOW and WHAT in only a couple words, lifestyle shots, and SKUs.

As you'll see from the next step, any clicks on these banners will show a high intent to view, cart, or purchase items within this category. Using the S.P.A.M. Strategy as the guide, you can now send follow-up messages about fire pits & decor to clickers of the fire pits & decor banner, creating more personalization opportunities and higher conversions.

## Stage #3: Click - Why Relationships Start Here

Remember the line about creatives without strategy being art and not advertising? Applied to email and SMS, creatives that are not designed to be clicked on are the equivalent of art. If you're reading this book, you're probably not focused on the art business (unless you sell art), so all creatives and messaging must focus on achieving one goal: the click.

**Every relationship starts with a click.** When a subscriber clicks on an email - or a shopper clicks on a Google search ad, Facebook ad, or display ad - that's an indication that they're interested in you and your message. And that's how great relationships are formed. Check out these relationship books below; it's all about clicking with someone.

Google built its entire business model around pay-per-click advertising because a click has high value. Amazon built its business around its 1-click checkout patent, showing how fewer clicks lead to a better shopping experience. Even now, the top SMS vendors like Attentive promote their two-tap signup option as the easiest and most frictionless method of list-building.

"When we write the history of electronic commerce, **the 1-Click patent** ... allowed Amazon to create a very strong position in the market."

— R. Polk Wagner,
University of Pennsylvania

**Every relationship starts with a click.** You may have worked out the finest context, copy, and creatives; without the click, it's just another message passed over in the inbox.

Design everything you do with the end goal of a click in mind. Create different templates for desktop and mobile to get higher clicks per device. Having a clear call-to-action (CTA) in your creatives are table stakes by now but think even bigger: what type of creatives, designs, and colors will maximize click rate?

Going beyond creatives, your send times and testing should all be geared around the highest likelihood to click. In fact, all our subject line testing is based around clicks. You may think that an open is the ultimate goal, but open tracking is quite convoluted these days due to iOS; generally, an open is easy to get, but the click is where the real value exists.

Check out the creatives above from DaSalla's (left) and Misen (right). Although the left creatives are well-designed with a great shot, I'm left to guess what this promotion really is. Is it about bowls, fruit, table settings, or something else? Not even sure what D Sale is, and with a three-second attention span, most consumers won't scroll to find out.

Compare it with the creative on the left - both cookware brands - and I'm very clear on the context, creative, offer, and call-to-action I need.

A click provides an opportunity for browsing, carting, and, obviously, converting. A sale is the ultimate outcome, of course, but browsing products can help refine your creatives dynamically. And customers can't browse unless they click.

Check out my inbox below with a ton of Wayfair emails. My single click into a Warehouse Clearance email showed I was interested in chandeliers - which I was at the time and ended up buying from them! That one click helped them launch a whole slew of chandelier emails my way to increase their chance of a conversion.

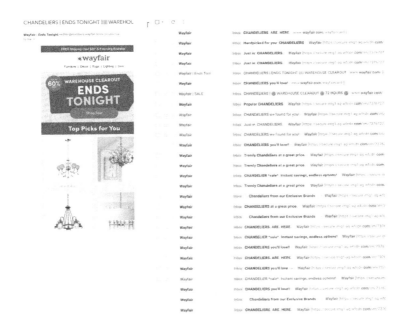

Every email is about chandeliers because that is where my Wayfair relationship started. I literally don't want to hear about any other products, and Wayfair KNOWS THAT because my click showed high intent. There's no intent about buying decisions until I click.

You'll learn more about this in the convert stage. But if you're not designing your emails to click, they're not going to convert at all. When it comes to seeing the impact of great context and superb creatives, remember just six words: every relationship starts with a click.

## Stage #4: Convert - Focus on the Destination

Now that you've excelled at getting clicks - and trust me, the clicks will explode compared to how you used to blast out - the key part of increasing sales is by landing the subscriber on the best place to convert.

This is where a solid linking strategy comes into play. Do a deep dive into your website pages, categories, anchor links, filters, sort capabilities, product variations, and so on.

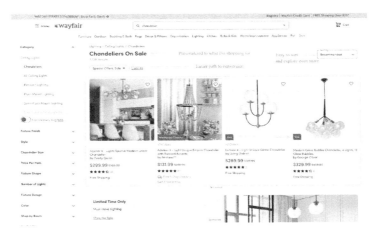

One page with great filtering and sorting can be a huge source of different links that show customers an entirely new assortment of products yet is extremely easy for you to scale.

Look at the Wayfair page above, specifically on the right. I got this email that said **"Chandeliers on Sale!"** and it was linked to the page shown. Note that this URL was filtered by "Recommended" and the URL string looks like this:

**https://www.wayfair.com/daily-sales/ds/chandeliers-youll-love-se18659.html**

If I simply re-sorted this page by "Highest Rated", I get an entirely different set of items with the five-star products at the very top. Therefore, if I sent an email about "Top-Rated Chandeliers" or an SMS about "Five-Star Chandeliers you have to see," the customer sees something entirely new, and the chances of converting increase.

What was the effort on your end? A simple creative change to **"Top-Rated Chandeliers!"** and putting a couple characters at the end of the URL (sortby=7, as shown below).

**https://www.wayfair.com/daily-sales/ds/chandeliers-youll-love-se18659.html?<u>sortby=7</u>**

The landing page is everything. If there's a mismatch between the email and website, your conversion rate will drop dramatically. If your URLs are the same every time, your conversion rate will tank on every successive send. If you don't use the numerous linking options inherent in your website, you'll get the click but not the sale.

This is where most marketers fall flat. They design the email, subject line, and creatives extremely well but fail to work on the landing page experience (usually because UX is an entirely different department).

The best part is that filtering, sorting, and categorizing can be owned by your team with little input from UX or merchandising. To start, create the landing pages yourself by tinkering with your URLs and measuring the conversion rates for every email; once you need more advanced landing pages, then at least you've made the case for extra help from other departments.

**1. SEARCH BY BRAND...**

**2. CHANGE THE SORT...**

**3. USE THE SEARCH URL IN YOUR CAMPAIGN!**

Another great method of personalizing emails to the user is by using the search bar. Check out the above search example from a hair and beauty brand. Imagine a subscriber started searching for the hair care and beauty brand Matrix but hasn't made a purchase yet. That search data is stored and can now be used to direct subscribers back to a whole bunch of Matrix items filtered in dozens of different ways.

I can show Matrix Top Rated, Matrix Best-Sellers, Matrix New Arrivals, Matrix Under $20, Matrix on Sale, Matrix Bundles, Matrix with Free Shipping, Matrix Bundles, and Matrix In-Stock. That's nine emails or texts I can send that all go back to the SAME URL with one minor URL change at the end. Here's an example with the only edit needed highlighted in bold and underlined:

Matrix Best-Sellers -
https://haircareandbeauty.com/search?**sort_by=best-selling**&q=matrix

Matrix on Sale -
https://haircareandbeauty.com/search?**sort_by=sale-descending**&q=m
atrix

Matrix in Stock -
https://haircareandbeauty.com/search?**sort_by=stock-descending**&q=
matrix

Hack your URLs and create a diverse amount of website destinations for your team to use, with each page providing a different experience for the customer. Match the creatives to the converting page, and your sales will take off with every touch.

***

Let's summarize. Our C-4 Design Playbook was created to help you excel at the hardest pillar of the S.P.A.M. Strategy: customer personalization. Using the four stages of Context, Creatives, Click and Convert as key phases in your design process, you'll create a highly persuasive and personalized design strategy that emotionally connects you with the customer. Focusing on the WHY and not just the HOW and WHAT will build customer trust, leading to the ultimate goal: better customer relationships.

We're in the home stretch, so it's important we focus on a major CRM topic: how to turn one-time buyers into lifetime buyers. Our proven Post-Purchase Hourglass approach will accomplish that and more.

**Free Video + Playbook: C-4 Design Playbook**

Go deeper into our C-4 Design Playbook on our free 45-minute webinar. In this video, I'll vividly walk you through the exact steps, concepts, and examples you'll need to implement this playbook successfully. In addition, I'll share our creative brief with you so your creative teams can stay aligned and on track. You can start the video by visiting HiFlyerDigital.com/C4Playbook.

# CHAPTER TEN

## The Post-Purchase Hourglass

Remember that statistic that says 74% of customers are one-time buyers? That statistic shows that most brands fail at the post-purchase experience. And there's a good analogy I learned from Joey Coleman, author of *Never Lose a Customer Again*, to explain this major gap.

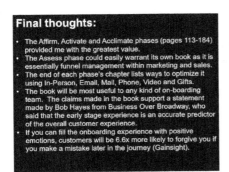

**Final thoughts:**

- The Affirm, Activate and Acclimate phases (pages 113-184) provided me with the greatest value.
- The Assess phase could easily warrant its own book as it is essentially funnel management within marketing and sales.
- The end of each phase's chapter lists ways to optimize it using In-Person, Email, Mail, Phone, Video and Gifts.
- The book will be most useful to any kind of on-boarding team. The claims made in the book support a statement made by Bob Hayes from Business Over Broadway, who said that the early stage experience is an accurate predictor of the overall customer experience.
- If you can fill the onboarding experience with positive emotions, customers will be 6.6x more likely to forgive you if you make a mistake later in the journey (Gainsight).

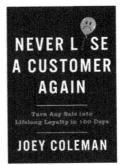

NEVER LOSE A CUSTOMER AGAIN

Turn Any Sale into Lifelong Loyalty in 100 Days

JOEY COLEMAN

Imagine you're dating someone, a common situation we can all relate to. You've dated, talked, and courted your date - let's call her Jill - through a wonderful relationship. You finally get the courage to propose and Jill agrees; you're officially engaged!

The wedding day arrives before you know it and after the rings, vows, and I do's, Jill marries the man of her dreams! Right after Jill walks down from the altar, though, elated at spending the rest of her life with you, she's quickly introduced to a new guy, Bill.

From here on, Bill will be responsible for continuing the relationship after the wedding date. Jill is not only shocked at the switcheroo but also hurt and angry about you ditching her after you crossed the finish line. Because Bill and Jill had no courtship, the relationship quickly dies.

My fiancé looks at me like this, I'm turning around.
#LoveIsBlind

Let's rewrite that love story in e-commerce terms: Jill is the customer, and you are the brand marketer that was responsible for courting her. You've run ads, sent emails and text messages, and automated your way into Jill's heart. And with a couple clicks and a credit card, Jill agreed to the purchase! As a marketer, your job is done; you've closed the deal, got her to say "I Do!" and you're on track for a bonus.

But for Jill, the customer, the lifelong marriage with your brand is just getting started… yet you're no longer there after the wedding day. Instead, Jill is introduced to Bill, the customer service rep she's never met, who's paid hourly, isn't aware of the previous courtship, and isn't incentivized in any way to build any relationship. Bill's mission: try to prevent Jill from communicating with him too often.

Bill's job is to answer your questions when it's not his lunch break, and, well, Jill has lots of questions about her new products. Jill feels a bit conned, let down, and kind of angry with this new relationship that she never asked for. Eventually, like that analogous marriage, Jill's relationship with your brand dies.

Millions of e-commerce brands have a terrible post-purchase experience, so it's no wonder that 74% of buyers are only one-time buyers. But instead of blaming it on customer service, who are thrust into a relationship they don't always know about nor commit to, I blame it on the marketers. And, as a marketer myself, I'm throwing myself into the blame game. There's a better way.

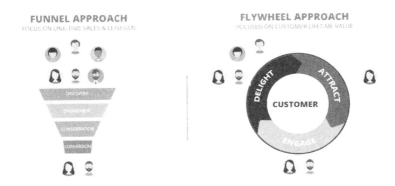

The overall blame game goes to the concept of the funnel. To marketers, customers are either in the top, middle, or bottom of the funnel; to the customer, that's not a very charming place to be, but marketers have to refer to the customer shopping stages in some way, I guess.

271

The problem with the funnel is that there's one endgame for marketers: get subscribers to the bottom of the funnel and convert them into customers.

In order to succeed at e-commerce, know this: the funnel is dead. The flywheel, the ongoing method of attracting, converting, and growing customers in loyalty and value, is the only viable way to scale your store.

The funnel is dead; long live the flywheel. I won't go into too much depth about how to use the customer flywheel for marketing purposes - that's for another future HiFlyer Digital book - but I want to help change your mindset a bit.

Focusing on funnel-based marketing leaves you with a bunch of one-time buyers; a flywheel-based marketing approach gives you a consistent path to growing customer lifetime value and attracting like-minded high-value customers.

Instead of discussing all the nuances of an overarching flywheel-based marketing approach to your business (shoot me an email at isaac@hiflyerdigital.com, and I'll be glad to send you my Funnel vs. Flywheel video), I can provide more immediate value to your brand by focusing on the very first opportunity to win over those one-time buyers: the post-purchase experience.

Focusing on the customer experience right after purchase - the 20% effort - will help you succeed at 80% of your customer lifetime value efforts.

I'm outlining a proven post-purchase framework that's worked extremely well for me. It's called the **Post-Purchase Hourglass**, and it works extremely well with your existing marketing funnel.

Let's dive into the four phases of the Post-Purchase Hourglass.

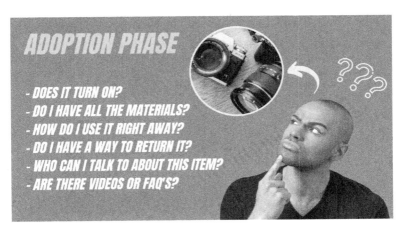

## Phase #1: Adoption - Onboard the Customer

These days, customer service and marketing must be closely intertwined. In fact, many e-commerce brands have a chief customer officer overseeing the marketing and customer service side of the business.

If you think about it, the same prospects you're targeting on Facebook and Google are the same customers reaching out to you on Messenger and WhatsApp after the purchase. Therefore, brands need a pre-purchase and post-purchase expert overseeing the full experience.

This is an important revelation. If marketing and customer service aren't communicating on a regular basis, you won't experience growth like the top 1%. Think about it: if marketers don't know WHY customers leave after their first purchase, they won't try to overcome that pain point in their pre-purchase marketing or post-purchase follow-ups.

On the flip side, if customer service doesn't know what marketing is selling, the reps won't have a good answer to the customer when they call in with questions, comments, or complaints about what they've been sold. The customer doesn't care who helps them; they just care about the product, service, or experience living up to their expectations.

One of our podcast guests, Chase Clymer, who hosts the Honest E-commerce Podcast - which I highly recommend you listen to - summarized why 90% of direct-to-consumer brands in the $1M range don't scale to the next level: they simply don't ask their customers for feedback on products, experiences, and areas of improvement! Instead, brands run off to catch the next customer and leave vital user-generated content, feedback, and, of course, lifetime loyalty on the table.

This is why the Adoption Phase is so important. This is the phase where marketers need to proactively address every challenge, question, and comment before the customer asks.

Let's use an example of a high-end mirrorless camera. I'm no photography expert, but cameras are a product I'm very familiar with. Imagine I ordered a $1,000 mirrorless camera, and I just got the order. I'm now at the stage where Jill was on her wedding day; I just committed to a whole new positive journey with your brand, product, and people. Your brand needs to keep the courtship going.

The Adoption Phase solves the following customer pain point: we need to help the customer unlock the complete value of their purchase as soon as possible.

When it comes to the mirrorless camera, customers like me have questions such as:

- Do I have everything I ordered in the box?
- Do I have my warranty information?
- How do I turn it on and start taking photos?
- Do I have an easy way to return it if need be?
- What should I do next?

Adoption means that you need to WOW the customer right out of the box (literally!) and anticipate their needs before they even ask. You're not selling them anything; you want to help them adopt the product and unlock its value immediately. Start this phase by positioning yourself as helpful within every touchpoint.

From a marketing perspective, you can have full control over the post-purchase email that shares links to FAQs, user manuals, or videos along with customer service touchpoints.

Think about it: most customers go straight to YouTube to learn how to use their new electronics. Instead of letting those customers slowly veer away from you, position your expert onboarding content in front of them.

Marketers can even control the box design, unboxing experience, and contents, all focused on the Adoption Phase. Your customer service team will thank you as they'll field fewer questions or complaints from customers, allowing them to excel in the pre- to post-purchase handoff.

You may ask: how many emails, texts or messages are necessary for this phase? To that, I'll respond that it differs per brand, and there's no wrong answer. Some industries - think high-end consumer electronics - need a good amount of attention and touchpoints in the Adoption Phase, while other industries - think grocery or replenishables - need fewer touches. Map out the number of critical touchpoints that must exist in order to create a truly successful handoff. One email may not be enough and ten emails / texts may be overkill, so try and orchestrate the key messages and put all secondary and tertiary lower in the email or landing pages.

From the consumer electronics perspective, our Adoption Phase touchpoints for camera buyers within the first 14 days included:

1. **Post-Purchase Survey** - we invited users to share feedback on their shopping experience, giving them a sense of ownership.
2. **Post-Purchase Thank You** - a personal note of thanks from our CEO with customized elements such as an animated Thank You gif and personalized name, product purchase and pertinent information.
3. **Let's Unbox Together** - post-delivery, we fired off an email giving them updates about what's in the box and what to do after you unbox the item (such as product registration and warranty).

4. **SMS Check-In text** - a text 12 hours after delivery asking how the delivery went and requesting any feedback; responses were answered by customer service instantly.

5. **The First Shot** - instead of an invite to explore our videos or blog, we positioned content around taking the first picture and what to do next, be it editing, social posting, sharing, or printing.

6. **Camera Concierge Introduction** - introduction to free personal imaging and video concierge; this was also a banner at the bottom of every email but merited a personal greeting as well.

7. **Join our Content Creator Community** - inviting users to join actual content creators in our private Facebook groups, as well as traditional social platforms, helping them learn from peers.

8. **Concierge Text Check-In** - a text from our concierge inviting camera customers to dialogue when needed.

9. **Trade-In Your Old Gear** - although slightly an upsell opportunity, for those who had old cameras, the new camera box was a useful way of sending back your old gear for cash or trade-in value. This was economical, easy to do, and eco-conscious all at once.

Quite an Adoption Phase! And within every email touchpoint, we had secondary messaging that focused on additional goals such as creating an account, joining our VIP program, and so on. These secondary messages will take on a bigger meaning in the Retention Phase.

Want a simple yet great example of an Adoption Phase? Take Apple and their iPhone. Ever noticed how the iPhone comes nearly fully charged, so you can immediately turn it on and start using it?

Before Apple started pre-charging its products, customers would have to charge their electronics or, worse, search for batteries to use immediately. How terrible does that sound right now! Apple knew that people wanted to use their iPhones immediately, so they pre-charged them to help customers adopt them quicker.

Map out your Adoption Phase so the customer can see value from their purchase immediately. The Adoption Phase is critical to delighting the customer right away. All communications, touchpoints (like the physical box and inserts), teams, and content should be orchestrated together to help the customer adopt the product. How long that phase lasts depends on the product. Overall, unlike Jill and Bill, the customer should experience a seamless transition between marketing and customer service.

# Phase #2: Retention - The Power of Value Stacking

I learned this next phase directly from our Chief Customer Officer. The Retention Phase focuses on the following hurdle: **the customer could've bought this product at numerous other stores, so it's critical to highlight the added value they unlock by buying from YOUR BRAND.**

This is where your blog, videos, experts, content, and social community come into play. In fact, after I bought my mirrorless camera, where did I logically go next? YouTube, of course, to watch videos on how to actually use the product quickly. As mentioned above, you need to position yourself as the go-to resource for those videos, tutorials, and guides.

Think about it. People buy products to achieve goals. Cameras are bought to create amazing content, brown shoes are bought to win the job interview, and running shoes are bought to stay fit and fabulous. The Retention Phase must position you as a partner in those goals.

But it goes beyond mere education. Think about the added value that you can add after every purchase. When I purchased the camera, I unlocked a personal photography concierge for 90 days as a result of my purchase, which gave me real photo expertise from experts without having to search around the internet.

I also unlocked rewards in the form of loyalty points that I could claim simply by registering my product. I could unlock additional points by following the brand's social platforms.

Of course, the brand I bought the camera from has a ton of great educational content. All that's left is positioning that content in front of me as part of the Retention Phase.

And the value stacking didn't end there. I also got an invitation to join a VIP club with premium content that I can unlock by logging into my account online.

I then got a unique discount for their sister brand that focused on photo printing, where I could bring my pictures to life on metal, canvas, and wood. Overall, the value I unlocked from my purchase was pretty immense, and, as a customer, I was excited to explore all the perks.

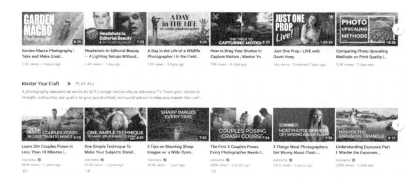

Now, in the Retention Phase, you've positioned your brand as the go-to source for great education and bonus perks you previously weren't aware of. Talk about customer delight!

Let's go even deeper: community. As a customer of mirrorless cameras, I've entered a community of other content creators who can help me become the best photographer I can be.

The Retention Phase should invite me to join the brand's social profiles, community chat platforms, or Facebook groups. I'm not only a customer anymore; I'm part of a community of mirrorless content creators! The result is that a customer will want to remain a part of that community and actually feel a loss by abandoning their peers, significantly improving customer retention.

Marketers need to find a brand's value and accentuate it in the Retention Phase. You don't have to have a huge amount of value but rather just relevant and differentiated value.

The more value, community and benefits, the less likely the customer is to abandon that value or community. In addition, you've positioned the mirrorless camera purchase as less of a product and more like an experience, giving your brand true differentiation.

I'll give a quick summary of the Retention Phase touches we rolled out; note that some got blended in the Adoption Phase as secondary messages, and some were stand-alone emails or texts:

1. **Join our VIP Club** - both our free and premium paid versions with exclusive value were presented to customers (most paid for it!)
2. **Personalized Videos + Content** - relevant content to products and brands they bought
3. **Discounts & Offers on Sister Brands** - as mentioned above, there were additional discounts for product rentals, trade-ins, and photo printing.
4. **Reward Points SMS** - each purchase unlocked a certain number of rewards, and customers had a chance to 2x and 3x the amounts with certain actions.
5. **Local / In-Store Benefits** - we had a bunch of opportunities for events, training sessions, and expert guidance for local customers.

Put the full power of your brand on display during the Retention Phase. Give your customers a "shock and awe" value experience that can't be matched by your competitors. Now, as you enter the Expansion Phase, you'll be in a better position for the upsell.

## Phase #3: Expansion - Maximize Their Purchase

The next stage is the Expansion Phase. By now, I've played around with my mirrorless camera, got all my questions answered, unlocked a lot of value that went above and beyond my purchase, and discovered a whole community of like-minded photographers to build a relationship with.

You've succeeded in adopting the customer and establishing your brand as a truly valuable resource. The Expansion Phase is now where you can begin upselling and cross-selling them products to expand the capabilities of the product.

The Expansion Phase is all about "expanding" on the original purchase and showing the customer how to extract the most value from their product with accessories, services, and add-ons.

For example, my mirrorless camera is great, but I could really use a sturdy tripod to keep my shots steady. And from what I saw in a tutorial video, I should probably consider getting a better lighting setup for a home studio. And from the thread in the private Facebook group, experts recommend a gimbal as well.

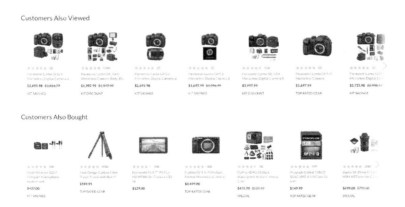

You're not selling me more products; you're helping me expand on my existing products and goals. In order to be the best photographer I can be, I will need to up my home studio, and because you've positioned your brand as a resource, I trust your resourceful product recommendations.

Note how there's little focus on upsell and cross-sell UNTIL you've onboarded, delighted, educated, and value-stacked the customer.

Up until the Expansion Phase, you've helped the customer adopt their product successfully, you've invited the customer into your tribe, you've showered them with incremental value not found anywhere else, and you've educated them on every benefit of the product.

Don't get me wrong; I put recommendations at the bottom of every post-purchase email. The only difference is that the Expansion Phase allows me to make those recommendations the primary message.

You now have the implicit permission to continue helping your customers maximize their purchase by selling additional products. Not only will this approach lead to an easier sell, you haven't broken any of the rapport established in previous phases.

This approach works for every business. In fact, in my agency, I do the exact same thing: once I hit our mutually-agreed-upon goals and establish a true commitment to helping my clients grow, I then begin to show them areas of improvement - such as SMS, SEO, or paid search - that could help them grow even more. Become a trusted partner and advisor, and you can expand any customer with additional products and services.

Although product upsells and cross-sells are most common, there may be other products or services that can get the lucrative second purchase and increase customer lifetime value. Here's a look at some of the areas I typically upsold:

1. **Recommended Accessories**
2. **Warranties & Gear Protection**
3. **VIP paid premium subscriptions**
4. **Trade-In Gear for Cash**
5. **Credit Cards & Financing**
6. **Product Rentals / Try-Before-You-Buy**
7. **Omni-Channel (get online buyers to buy in-store)**

The Expansion Phase is clearly focused on getting the customer to expand on their purchase by buying additional products and services.

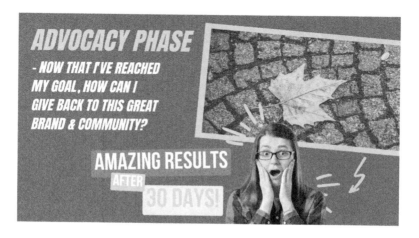

## Phase #4: Advocacy - How to Ask for Feedback

The final Advocacy Phase is where you have a chance to ask the customer to give back to you. You've helped the customer adopt their product, access all the value your brand offers and maximize their purchase further. Now you can ask for their review, feedback or referral.

There's nothing more important than a great referral. Every satisfied customer has a tribe of friends and family with like-minded interests that can be influenced your way. However, if you ask for a product review or referral before you've gone through the first three post-purchase phases, you'll waste your request and won't get another opportunity.

I would say a majority of brands ask for a review or try to upsell a customer before they even have a chance to get the product delivered or onboarded! And ever noticed how, after checkout, you get a pop-up that says refer a friend? Why would anyone refer a friend before they know how the purchase experience goes? Quite a presumptuous, ridiculous, and ill-timed request.

Don't waste the opportunity for a truly great referral by requesting it too early. The Advocacy Phase comes only after you've met the customers' expectations, exceeded their value expectations, maximized their purchase, and shown commitment to helping them achieve their goals.

Now is when you can ask for a review or a referral. This is where you obtain a lot more raised hands and willing participants. Your customers will be willing to share their experience with others, leave a review, answer questions, and dialogue on social media.

You can also use this opportunity to get their feedback on how to improve services and fulfillment. This user-generated feedback is extremely valuable and helps you constantly improve your offerings without expensive trial and error.

Most brands assume that the entire Advocacy Phase revolves around leaving a product review, but it clearly goes deeper than that. For every product review you actually receive, there are 10x more people behind the scenes who will talk to friends and family about your brand and products.

The value of a great product review goes beyond just the five stars on your homepage. You can leverage the actual user-generated content for the C-4 Design Playbook and create a real-life contextual message for your campaigns. Use the customer reviews for great storytelling about how your product fills a need, or bring the review to your R&D team for insights on where to improve products or services. A great review has numerous applications for your business.

The key is to not ask for it too quickly. The Advocacy Phase is the last phase in the Post-Purchase Hourglass because it is the culmination of a great customer experience. If you've excelled in the first three phases, then you can feel confident that the Adoption Phase will yield personalized and rewarding reviews!

Some examples of the advocacy requests we had in the Adoption Phase included:

1. **Product Review**
2. **Google & Facebook Review**
3. **Questions & Answers requests**
4. **Hashtags with pictures of product in use**
5. **Net Promoter Score survey**

A customer advocate is the highest level of customer satisfaction. Don't squander it by asking too early.

*\*\*\**

You may ask: what's the length or timing of the Post-Purchase Hourglass experience? The answer depends on the product; the bigger the price point, the longer it's going to take for them to go through the Post-Purchase Hourglass experience.

For example, if I bought a camera, I may not buy another camera for a year, but I may buy a smaller item sooner, like a memory card or gimbal. On the flip side, if I'm buying a stick of gum, I may want a stick of gum in a week from now. The time frame all depends on the type of product.

These are the four phases of the Post-Purchase Hourglass, where each successive touchpoint stacks additional education, expertise, service, and value. With every touchpoint, the customer almost feels obligated to make a repeat purchase and give back to the brand that has over-delivered on their expectations. With every positive review and referral, your customers will grow in lifetime value and end up being your most passionate advocates.

REPEAT BUYER VALUE

ONE-TIME BUYER
$110 Annual Value
Identified Category Preference
Clarified Channel Preference
Measurable Acquisition Value

REPEAT BUYER
$864 Annual Value
Improved Loyalty
Multi-Channel Preference
Enhanced Lifetime Value

7x | 9x | 25%
AV increase | LTV increase | jump in AOV

For most brands, the immediate KPI for the Post-Purchase Hourglass would be a repeat purchase. For a longer-term view, you should track the predicted customer lifetime value to determine how valuable a 2x buyer is compared to a 1x buyer.

From my experience, you can expect to see around a 600% increase in customer lifetime value just by turning a 1x buyer into a 2x buyer. Right above is a snapshot of what a repeat buyer meant to one of our clients.

\*\*\*

The Post-Purchase Hourglass will help you tackle the biggest e-commerce challenge of all: turning one-time buyers into lifetime buyers. But the Hourglass is just the starting point of your retention strategy - retention is an organizational-wide and ever-changing strategy - yet it can be fully executed using email and SMS as the key customer touchpoints.

Aside from turning 1x buyers into 2x buyers, you can multiply this automation to turn 2x buyers into VIP buyers or focus on turning non-buyers into 1x buyers. Additional CRM goals should be focused on customer win-back, customer churn, risk-of-churn, loyalty, and other customer migrations that grow lifetime value and profits.

Now that I've unlocked the S.P.A.M. Strategy and shared how the Post-Purchase Hourglass is the most lucrative use case for it, let's complete the last part of this book: the additional automations every e-commerce brand needs and how they can each be improved with the S.P.A.M. Strategy.

**Free Video: Using Email, SMS & Social for Retention**

Social media, social proof and user generated content plays a vital role in keeping customers loyal and growing lifetime value. Take your customer retention strategy to the next level by orchestrating email, SMS and social media - paid and organic - to work together in the pursuit of customer loyalty. On our "Turn One-Time Buyers into Lifetime Buyers" webinar, I'm joined by Chavie Fuchs, our social media expert, and together we illustrate how to win the hearts and minds of customers using email, SMS and social media.. You can watch the full video recap by visiting HiFlyerDigital.com/retention/

# CHAPTER ELEVEN

## Top 10 Email & SMS Automations

No book about email, SMS and CRM is complete without doing a rundown of the top e-commerce automations.

One of my agency's core values is "work smart, not hard," and we embody that value through marketing automation. Our goal for our clients is to create a profitable, predictable, and sustainable revenue stream for their business; email and SMS automations are how we achieve that goal.

You can certainly find these top ten automations out there with a basic Google search. Most ESPs even provide an "out-of-the-box" framework for some of these that you can turn out automatically; some are good, some are bad, and some are too basic.

What I'm going to do in this chapter is dive into the top 10 e-commerce automations through two different lenses:

1. How to leverage the S.P.A.M. Strategy to truly personalize and humanize these automations for your customers
2. How to think more macro about what these automations can and should do for your business.

## Automation #1: Welcome

**Goal: welcome new subscribers to your email list through a series of emails that nurture, onboard, and position your brand as a resource for a long-term relationship.**

A Welcome series is your opportunity to introduce your brand, show new subscribers what to expect from your email program, and provide potential customers with the resources they need to move through the buying process.

## Discounts Work (If You Think Long Term)

If you can swing a discount, that's the quickest way to get a purchase. Can't swing it? Think about this: the lifetime value of a customer vs. subscriber is a huge swing. One of the brands I worked with attributed a $12 lifetime value to every email they acquired, but when that subscriber made a purchase, the value of that customer jumped to $127 lifetime value. If a discount turns a subscriber into a customer quickly, that's a long-term benefit for your brand. The likelihood of purchase shrinks dramatically every day a subscriber remains on your list without purchasing.

## New Subscribers vs. New Customers

Be sure to trigger a Welcome series to new subscribers, not new customers. The journey of a new subscriber is different than a new customer. As explained in the Post-Purchase Hourglass, new customers are onboarded; new subscribers are nurtured. Big difference. Not only is it a nightmare for customer service to try and explain that the 15% OFF discount for new subscribers can't be applied to purchases already processed (I've had to deal with headaches like that!), but the journey is entirely different as explained in chapter ten.

**Focus on Story-Selling**

Some brands like to focus their entire Welcome series on content. Having A/B tested hundreds of Welcome emails, a content-only workflow is a missed opportunity. Customers don't sign up to your list to read or watch videos; they have YouTube and Google for that. They sign up for offers, first-look opportunities, and curiosity about what everyone else is buying.

Look at Nike's story-selling with an invite to their club and trending items right below it. They know subscribers want to buy what everyone else is buying, so they welcome you to the club. For their subscribers, it's not just about the discount; it's about the membership.

As such, you can tell your story and nurture new subscribers into your world - such as a YouTube video about your mission - but don't be afraid to show personalized dynamic picks in every email. That's what we call "story-selling" - share your story but sell at the same time. These days, where commoditized items are sold by numerous competitors, having a core story, mission, and values is indeed a differentiator; subscribers, however, came to your website to buy.

Having tested hundreds of Welcome email combinations, my best-performing went like this:

1. **Welcome Offer + Personalized Picks + Shop by Category**
2. **Our Story Video + Offer Reiteration + Favorite Picks**
3. **New Arrivals + Offer Reiteration + Shop by Category**

4. **Best-Sellers + Offer Reiteration + Shop by Category**
5. **Offer Reiteration + Personalized Picks + Shop by Category**
6. **Last Chance Welcome Offer + Personalized Picks + Shop by Category**

I didn't dance around the lead nurturing by having separate emails for join our social media (that can be in Touch 2) or visit our blog (also in Touch 2), or customer service email (that's in all emails under the value proposition section) because new subscribers mainly want to know what everyone is buying and if they can be first to buy as well.

They just need a point in the right direction, which is what New Arrivals and Best-Sellers achieve. The personalized picks is textbook S.P.A.M. Strategy; if they're browsing items, those items will show up in the email automatically.

Sell the story, and your customers are more likely to pay full price and feel more invested in your brand. Remember, customers can get the same products everywhere (half of them are all made in the same factory overseas!), but they'll stay for the brand, mission, and experience.

## Automation #2: Cart Abandon

**Goal: regain lost revenue from customers who abandoned their cart before purchase through a series of reminder emails and texts.**

According to eMarketer, 70% of e-commerce shopping carts are abandoned. Because the cart abandoner is nearly at the finish line, I can pretty much guarantee that abandoned cart emails will be one of the most profitable and highest converting emails you send. In some cases, your abandoned cart email campaign will be your most profitable campaign.

An abandoned cart email campaign enables you to reach out to customers who have demonstrated high buying intent. So, you'll often win the sale. That's why abandoned cart campaigns are so profitable. And, since they're so profitable, abandoned cart emails are an absolute necessity for e-commerce email marketing.

**Multiple Emails Aren't Annoying. They're Personalized.**

Don't be afraid to send a series of emails to recover abandoned carts. You should certainly test the exact number of emails to send, but don't shy away from sending multiples.

I sometimes get eye rolls for this and brands screaming that too many emails are annoying and invasive. Here's my response to that: **what is the alternative?**

Let's be honest; you're going to email them something anyway! And most likely, that email will be another unpersonalized batch mailing. So why not opt to send them a super-personalized, super-relevant email that has a higher likelihood of converting?

Remember, the money is in the follow up. Obviously, when the purchase occurs, you end the flow, but follow-up cart abandon emails will capture those lost sales better than any campaign.

**Solve Why They Abandon in the First Place**

The number one reason why customers abandon their cart is surprise costs at checkout, such as unanticipated shipping costs, tax increases, and the like. Forcing customers to create an account or too many steps in the checkout process are reasons two and three, respectively.

Obviously, you want to try and overcome those with a cart abandon email. But the real way to solve cart abandon is by finding out how to keep customers from abandoning in the first place. An email or SMS is a nice way to recover carts, but you have a bigger abandonment problem to solve.

Even small changes - such as a banner that highlights "You're only $XX away from free shipping" or "stock is running low, complete your order" is a great way to overcome abandonment problems. Study the checkout experiences of your favorite brands. Use HotJar, a website heatmap tool, to learn where the checkout hurdles are and test different checkout experiences for your customers.

**Boost Your Cart Recovery with a Cross-Channel Approach**

Another great way to go macro on this automation is by using a cross-channel approach, with the first pass going to email. Remember when we said that maybe 50% of the people abandoning our cart are actually subscribers? Well, what do you do with the other 50% that 1) you can't identify or 2) are unsubscribed?

This is where a great cross-channel strategy will help with your cart recovery. If a cart abandoner is subscribed to your email list, give email a first pass and send a cart email. Remember, email is a free, high ROI channel so leveraging it first is the most profitable option.

If a customer is not subscribed, you have two options: send them an SMS if they're subscribed or run a Facebook retargeting campaign. Both channels are more expensive than email, but what choice do you have? There's no better campaign to spend some dollars on than a cart abandon retargeting.

Let's go one step deeper and think about the customer journey. Assuming that 50% of your cart abandon emails get opened, and 10% get clicked, that leaves 50% of your retargeting efforts missed or ignored.

For that disengaged population, there's little reason to send another email that will be missed, so send them an SMS. The more marketing channels a customer is subscribed to, the higher chance of converting the sale.

## Automation #3: Browse Abandon

**Goal: turn window shoppers into customers through a nurture campaign focused on variety, content, and education.**

Customers are always window shopping. Browse abandonment emails turn these window shoppers into customers through highly-personalized email touches that "answer all their questions" at once.

Similar to cart abandon, send multiple emails that will turn browsers into customers or, at the very least, add-to-carters. The timing of your emails should start on the same day but don't wait three or four days to send the next one; browsers are in buying mode now, and you don't want to miss the opportunity to help fill their needs.

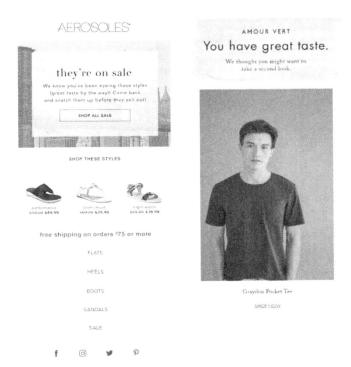

You may say that too many emails will anger them, right? The data shows otherwise. We've established by now that personalization is how you become more helpful, relevant, and useful to every customer... and then they'll want to hear from you more often. Here are some tips to help amp up that browsing personalization.

**Focus on Pleasure Points & Pain Points**

Your browse abandon approach should focus on nurturing window-shoppers to cross the finish line. To make that happen, you need to have a full repertoire of marketing tools in your arsenal. These tools are known as content, and they come in two forms: A+ content and user-generated content (UGC).

A+ content allows you to expand the view and perspective of the product beyond the product page; think like videos of the product in action or hands-on reviews from staff experts. User-generated content includes reviews, testimonials, and questions / answers, which essentially means you get positive feedback from others to sell for you.

Compile your best content to help guide the customer over the finish line. Focus on the content that will overcome their pain points and hesitations while simultaneously accentuating the pleasure points of having the item.

Using our example of brown Oxford shoes, here are a few secondary and tertiary banners or blocks to include in your browse abandon emails:

- **Reviews of the brown Oxford shoes**
- **Video of styles with the shoes**
- **Buying guides that include the shoes**
- **Direct links to Q&A about the fit, look & size**
- **Reminders about free shipping or free returns**
- **Reviews about your brand overall**
- **Easy CTAs for call / chat / SMS help**

Per the Multiplication pillar of the S.P.A.M. Strategy, the content should be scalable across multiple products and categories. Having great content for one product line is great, but if you can't scale it, you'll miss selling points for other products. Your designers or coders should be able to combine all these variables into a cohesive-looking email. Since browse abandon should be a series of multiple email touches, you can opt to stagger all your content over multiple emails or touch on all of it in every email.

I've found the most success using all our content in every email, tracking what content block gets clicked the most (aside from the product), and then optimizing the very first email to focus on the highest clicked area. For example, if a customer primarily clicks on reviews of the product, my first email will be edited to say "Rave Reviews for {{Product Name}}!" increasing the open, click, and conversion rates from the very start.

**Use dynamic recommendations everywhere.**

If a customer is browsing an item without carting or buying it, this should signal that the customer is in the consideration phase. For many customers, price or selection may be holding them back. Dynamic recommendations allow you to position more appealing items that are perfect for their price range, taste, size, and color.

For example, I may have browsed those brown Oxford shoes, but if my size was out of stock, I'd simply keep browsing. I wouldn't cart a shoe that doesn't fit me, right? However, if I knew that there was a similar brown shoe in stock, I'd be more likely to 1) click, 2) browse, 3) cart, 4) buy. Dynamic recommendations help you position more relevant products in front of the customer during a high-intent buying time.

Remember, the path to purchase is not always linear. Showing product recommendations enables the customer to shop for their product of interest as well as discover additional products they may have missed.

**Track High-Level Intent vs. Low-Level Intent**

Some brands think window shopping isn't a high-intent buying signal, while other brands see browsing behavior as the ultimate high-intent signal. Find out for yourself. You can optimize your browse abandonment campaigns by testing different browse thresholds and behavioral triggers. For example, segment high-intent customers who are:

- Viewing the same item more than once.
- Browsing multiple items in the same product category
- Clicking on a certain product in an email.
- Searching your site for a specific category or product.
- Three browse sessions vs. one browsing session

By segmenting out your browsing customers, you can determine which customers are browsing to buy and which are simply window shopping and how that impacts your email engagement and conversion.

## Automation #4: Category Browse

**Goal: expand beyond browse abandon by introducing new category options for the customer to discover.**

Category browse is the best automation you've never heard of. Hardly any brand tries it, no ESP talks about it, and only the top 1% of the 1% actually create it. It took me years of browsing, carting, and shopping to unlock the mentality of category browse and perfect the data necessary to make this part of your top five automations.

Category browse is best compared to an actual window shopper in-store. Think about a person browsing a pair of brown Oxford shoes in-store. You, being the salesperson, try to sell them these shoes by throwing all your content, reviews, FAQs, and every other sales tactic at them. This approach is the e-commerce equivalent of browse abandon. After all that, still no sale.

The difference between store commerce and e-commerce, though, is that the salesperson in-store attempts to show the customer other shoes in the aisle; maybe something else is a fit. After all, the customer is still in the aisle, came in to buy something, and is in consideration mode.

Why talk up a random shirt sale or an upcoming sneaker BOGO when you know the customer came for shoes? They certainly didn't come in for shirts. The salesperson in-store knows this and attempts to guide customers into new shoe styles while they're in the aisle.

When it comes to e-commerce, though, most brands throw people back into the day-to-day campaigns (like the shirt sale or sneaker BOGO) if browse abandon doesn't convert.

That's a missed opportunity because the customer is still trying to get a pair of shoes (but obviously not THOSE shoes). Take the time to "walk customers through the aisle" using a category browse automation.

Category browse is all about discovery. Your browse abandon program ran for the brown Oxford shoes, so instead of throwing your subscribers back into your day-to-day campaigns, slowly walk them through additional shoes and introduce them to shoes that they may have overlooked.

Because Wayfair is my favorite brand to watch for email, SMS and CRM, I had to screenshot my inbox for you.

Do you see how my chandelier browsing triggered more than just a browse abandon email for my product? In my inbox, there are emails focused on handpicked chandeliers, chandeliers I'll love, popular chandeliers, chandeliers on clearance, and on and on for at least 9+ touches.

Wayfair even knew that I was in "home improvement mode" and sent me a 'top brands for home improvement projects email! Guess what was the first category within the home improvement' email? The chandeliers category. Guess what I ended up buying? A chandelier!

This isn't the first time Wayfair excelled in walking me slowly through their aisles; check out what they sent me when I was browsing futons:

Nearly a month of emails focused on the category I was browsing helped me DISCOVER more products and options that I overlooked or didn't know existed.

Too many emails, you say? I have three answers for you:

1. **Relevant emails and texts are not annoying; they're personalized, helpful, and educational.** Compare the

unsubscribe rate to your batch mailings, and you'll see the power of marketing relevancy.

2.  **What's the alternative?** You'll just end up sending that customer another batch and blast campaign that's totally irrelevant to them, let's be honest. So, if you're going to email or text them anyway, why not make it a super relevant email or text?

3.  I've spoken to some of Wayfair's top data scientists and, trust me, **they run numerous tests on their email lists**. I can assure you that if they're sending this many touches, they've already proven that the approach works. My goal is to get you to the level of the top 1%, so this is a good brand to keep an eye on!

So, how do you achieve great category browse automations? Use these super-simple yet highly effective tactics.

**Use product filtering and sorting in your campaigns.**

Check out the below screenshot from B&H Photo. In the green highlighted areas, they have dozens of category permutations that can be shown to a customer browsing a Sony Mirrorless Camera. For example:

- Sony Cameras In-Stock
- Sony Mirrorless Camera New Releases
- Sony Mirrorless Camera Best-Sellers
- Sony Mirrorless Camera Deals
- Sony Mirrorless Cameras In-Store
- Sony Mirrorless Cameras + Free Shipping
- Sony Mirrorless Cameras Under $1,000

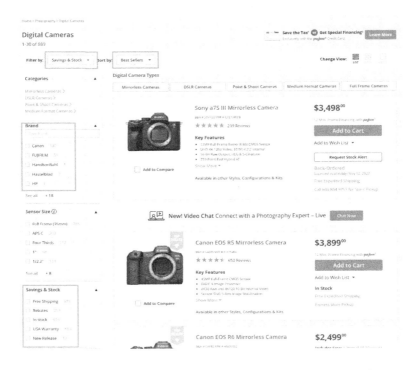

Every filter can be a new email touch or a block in a larger email. I can even remove the word "Sony" and have dozens of additional touches after that. Your website is full of hidden gems, yet, like a Google search, most customers won't get past the page 1 listings. Great product filters and faceted search will help your customers discover more products to love, increasing conversions and positioning your brand as a helpful expert.

**Maintain clean product categorization and data dictionary.**

Most brands have dozens of product categories that are a complete mess. One product I used to work with - a Leica M Series Digital Camera - was nested under the top-level category of 1) Leica Digital Cameras, yet the Leica M Series Lens was nested under three categories - 1) Accessories, 2) Lenses, and 3) Leica Lenses. One would think that a Leica M Series Lens would have a top-level category of Leica Lenses, just like Leica Digital Cameras, but clearly, the categorization was incongruous.

Why does that matter? Think back to the Multiplication phase of the S.P.A.M. Strategy. If I built a Category Browse automation with the top-level category showing "Leica Digital Camera Best-Sellers," I wouldn't be able to scale that automation to other categories.

For example, everyone who browsed a Leica Lens would only see "Accessories Best-Sellers," which wouldn't be as personalized. The top-level category for each product - Leica Digital Cameras and Accessories, respectively - don't match up well, and it's a bad customer experience. And this is just one example at a glance; there could be thousands of other products miscategorized or misaligned.

Most brands focus their energy on the user experience when shopping yet don't think about the cleanliness of the data for their marketing channels. I don't blame them; sometimes, you have to get a new category launched quickly, or a new collection put online at a moment's notice.

But know the ramifications of good data hygiene. Data cleanliness is why Wayfair excels in their email, SMS and CRM automations like Category Browse... and other brands struggle to scale beyond one or two touches.

Take the time to audit your product catalog, ensure a cohesive category structure and create a data dictionary of every product data point (as we covered in the Foundations chapter). Use collections, filters, variables, and other product data points correctly instead of "winging it" to get a sale or offer going. A great data dictionary will enable you to multiply your automations to the next level.

## Automation #5: Post-Purchase

We dove into the Post-Purchase Hourglass in the previous chapter, so I won't dive into it again in depth. I will remind you, however, that the 80/20 Rule is the only way to scale your e-commerce store. The more one-time buyers you can turn into lifetime buyers, the more you will grow.

Once you launch and perfect your Post-Purchase Hourglass, the only addition I can make here is to start thinking about a cross-channel and omni-channel expansion. Most marketing channels operate in a silo and don't always communicate well with each other.

Let's face it: the email team doesn't want to miss their revenue goals by sharing attribution with social media, and the search team doesn't want to have ad budgets shrunk because email is a higher ROI channel.

By involving the search, social, customer service, and store teams in growing customer lifetime value, you'll create an orchestrated marketing omni-presence that surrounds the customer with value, education, and offers everywhere they look. A rising tide lifts all ships.

## Automation #6: Churn & Risk of Churn

**Goal: win back customers who have not bought from you in a while, as well as prevent customers from leaving in the first place.**

I group Churn and Risk-of-Churn together because they're both critical to keeping customers loyal. In fact, winning a customer back from their churn stage is 8x more difficult than preventing them from churning in the first place.

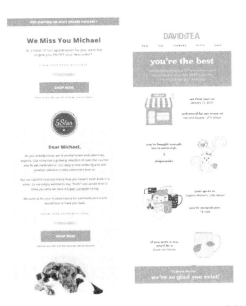

Churn essentially means that a customer has fallen off their expected buying cycle. Subscription-based e-commerce brands are the most familiar with this: if a customer bought four times in four months and then skipped a month, that customer is at risk of churning. If the customer skipped another month, that customer has churned.

The timetable for what churn looks like is different for every industry; in the consumer electronics industry, when a customer didn't buy at least once in the last 180 days, they were only considered at risk of churn due to the high AOV and longevity of the products.

For a D2C food kit delivery service, the risk of churn may be as short as a few weeks. That churn window differs per industry.

The key takeaway is this: most brands focus more energy on gaining customers than on keeping and growing customers, and that's a huge missed opportunity. A healthy churn and risk-of-churn workflow will help you reduce customers from leaving and even win back the ones you thought were gone forever. Here are a few things to help you perfect these churn automations.

**Know your numbers.**

Guessing when a customer is at risk of churn is not a strategy. Dive into your purchasing patterns and get a good benchmark for when customers tend to drop off after purchase.

You don't need to focus on every category line right now; start with an overall glance. Set up a few evergreen segments in your ESP or CRM to track buyers by lifetime purchase and keep an eye on them weekly for peaks and valleys.

Get to know the words RFM modeling. Recency, frequency, and monetary (RFM) analysis will give you a good look at what customers buy, how often, how recent, and how much they spend.

You may find that the more they buy, the longer they stay. But don't guess at it: you can use Excel or any number of online tools - as well as some ESP-based predictors - to get you started on knowing your numbers.

**Prevention is 80% of the cure.**

As mentioned above, preventing a customer from churning is 8x more effective than trying to win the customer back once they've churned.

Focus all your efforts on prevention. Let's take an example: if a jewelry shop knows a customer has shopped 1x a month for the last four months but didn't purchase this month at all (month 5), focus your entire next month (month 6) on preventing them from missing another month. Campaigns such as Customer Appreciation Week, We Miss You, and 3x Rewards do wonders for making a customer feel special and bringing them back onto their traditional buying pattern.

Don't settle for one-and-done campaigns. Focus entire weeks on this strategy because prevention is 80% of the cure. After giving your email channel the first pass at churn prevention, triangulate your risk-of-churn campaigns with SMS & social media.

It will be more cost-effective for you to spend some ad dollars to keep this customer than it does to acquire a new customer. The key to triangulating your risk-of-churn campaign is to make your campaign creatives and messaging consistent across the board. Align the search, social and UX team and pursue a cross-channel churn prevention strategy. No more marketing silos when it comes to winning back customers; it's all hands on deck!

Once they've churned, you'll have a harder time winning them back. There's no major difference between a risk-of-churn campaign and a churn campaign; they're nearly exactly the same. The only difference is prevention, so if they've churned, try running similar campaigns to win them back.

You may have to spend more on paid media to get their attention, but with the right offer, segmentation, personalization, and channel orchestration, you stand a good chance of winning back some of your high-value customers.

## Automation #7: Re-Engagement

**Goal: re-engage your disengaged subscribers and get them to engage with your emails, SMS, and brand.**

There's a difference between churn and re-engagement. Churn and risk-of-churn, sometimes called reactivation, focuses on winning back a dormant customer.

Re-engagement is when you get a subscriber who hasn't opened or clicked an email in a set period of time to engage with you again. You should only be communicating with subscribers who are actually invested in your channel. If they aren't, invite them to another medium - like SMS or social - and start thinking about sunsetting them from email.

Worried about losing revenue by deleting subscribers? I feel your pain, but I've got two words for you: Pareto Principle. In every case, most of your email revenue will come from your engaged subscriber base only, be it 30 days engaged, 5 days engaged, or anywhere in between. The subscribers with a 5% open rate and .5% click rate aren't doing much for your business. Give re-engagement a go, and then let them go.

**Disengaged subscribers affect deliverability.**

Removing the unengaged subscribers keeps your deliverability rates high. If certain subscribers have not opened emails in the last 60 days, 90 days, 180 days, or any predetermined timetable you have, send one last email and take them off your list.

Having disengaged subscribers on your list means that they don't want to hear from you. Sending them more emails may lead to higher spam complaints, dropping your deliverability rates. Even if some of those dormant subscribers do click, risking high spam complaints is not a great tradeoff for you. Avoid getting flagged by your ESP or even Gmail by sunsetting dormant subscribers.

**Re-engage users with a one-click message**

Every relationship starts with the click. Your re-engagement emails should focus on that one option: click. Using the above email screenshots as an example, note how terse and basic they are. Subscribers can only do one thing: click or not click. That one data point will tell you if they're still in or if they simply lost interest.

Even better, as we know from before, a simple click unlocks data and gets the customer back to your website, at which point they're browsing and viewing and even buying. All because you've asked them if they want to stay without dancing around it. I've seen a decent amount of revenue come from re-engagement campaigns, not a massive amount because they're quite dis-engaged, but enough to justify having a one-click email. This isn't yet the time to invite them to social or SMS or call customer service; just a one-click "are you in or not" call to action will determine their engagement level.

**Don't Delete. Just Re-Assign.**

Imagine you deleted a subscriber from your database, and then 30 days later, they abandoned their cart. You had an opportunity to trigger a highly engaged cart abandon email to them and missed out because you deleted them!

I've never found success by deleting a subscriber. Instead, I re-tag them as Dormant or Cull or, in some playful cases, the

Walking Dead. These are subscribers, after all, and they may not be engaged right now. When Black Friday or Cyber Monday comes along, though, they may buy 10x what your usual customers buy.

Instead of deleting, keep their data there but avoid day-to-day campaigns to that population. In fact, I used to send the Cull population one batch email every 60 days just to let them know we're still here and keep their ISP familiar with our brand.

The campaigns I sent them were large-scale campaigns such as Memorial Day, Labor Day, and BFCM, seasons where people expect to get a ton of messages. These campaigns won't result in a ton of revenue, but some emails did re-engage the Cull population, triggering high-performing cart and browse automations and getting some value from them.

In addition, you can use your ESP as a hub for all marketing channels in lieu of a customer data platform (CDP). Send your dormant subscribers to Facebook and Google every week and run a campaign against them.

There are marketing options that go beyond sending emails and texts. Unless your ESP budget is very tight, don't delete the data. Just reassign them, avoid mailing them often and touch them every 60 to 90 days max.

## Automation #8: Search Abandon

**Goal: use customer auto-fill search data to power a discovery-focused, product-based nurture series**

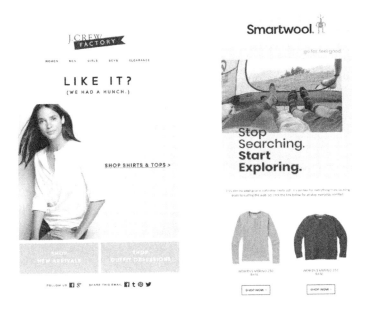

Sounds like a lot of buzzwords, right? Well, I'll break it down a little simpler. 43% of customers go straight to a website's search bar, making it the most trafficked place on your website. You can thank Google for training people to search for stuff rather than browse around at first glance. Similar to a Google search, your website search bar generally provides auto-fill options when a visitor begins typing.

For example, if I start typing the words "Nike" on Nordstrom's website, I have multiple auto-fill options such as "Nike shoes", "Nike for women", "Nike Air Force 1", and more. Depending on what I click on, I get taken to the PDP, PLP, or maybe even a brand page dedicated to Nikon.

If I go to the Nike Air Force 1 PDP page, look at the item and then abandon, I'll probably get a Browse Abandon series because I viewed a product. But what if I clicked on Nike for women or Nike shoes? I obviously wouldn't get a product Browse Abandon because I didn't view a product; I'm still in search mode. But I showed a very high-intent buying signal through my search history. Most brands overlook that buying signal, and Search Abandon fills that gap.

Search Abandon is another automation that most brands sleep on. Shoppers in search mode are low-hanging fruit; they haven't settled on an item yet, but they're still in hunt mode and could use some guidance.

Think of it similarly to a Google search; customers are in search mode, and you simply need to "push" them in your direction (unlike Facebook, where you have to "pull" them from their chill-mode scrolling and video-watching behavior).

A Search Abandon workflow identifies a high-intent prospect and gives the customer a relevant starting point for their search.

So, what do you send once they've searched? Exactly what you as a customer would want to receive: personalized recommendations, categories, and content that will help them discover new and relevant items. Search Abandon is one of the top-performing automations you can have, and it's quite similar to Category Browse. Here's how to excel with this automation.

**Map out the Abandon logic.**

With all these Abandon automations running, it's easy to miss a step and accidentally send a redundant email to a poor subscriber. For example, if I searched for a category, I would be eligible for a Search Abandon email.

If I went to an actual product after the search, I would stand to get a Browse Abandon email. And if I carted that item, I'm eligible for a Cart Abandon email. I'm eligible for three high-performing emails, right? Yet not only would it be a terrible customer experience to send all three to me in the span of a 24-hour period, it would also be a missed opportunity to send me the lowest impact email of the three!

Here's where the abandon logic plays a major role, so let's break it down:

1) **Customer searches for Nike shoes**
   a) **Did they browse an item?**
      i) **Yes**
         (a) **Did they cart an item?**
         (b) **(Yes**
                 (i)    **Send Cart Abandon**
         (c) **No**
                 (i)    **Send Browse Abandon**
      ii) **No**
         (1) **Send Search Abandon**

Rinse and repeat that logic on the next send as well to ensure that the highest performing email - and most personalized email - goes to the customer at all times.

**Bring in Auto-Filled Search Data, Not All Search Data.**

The biggest roadblock to turning on a Search Abandon campaign is the lack of auto-fill search data. Many brands don't have auto-fill in their search bar and run the risk of sending vague search results into their ESP.

Try triggering an email when someone mistypes Lenses to be Leses; the links, subject line and content all break down, and the email becomes incoherent (happens ALL THE TIME). Implement auto-fill into your search bar, so you have actionable data available to you. There's a reason why Google built that auto-fill logic, and it's a major part of internet life these days.

A second roadblock to turning on Search Abandon is that some brands don't store the search terms anywhere, which is clearly a missed opportunity. Take the time to power search data into your ESP consistently - weekly or, even better, daily - and be sure to power in auto-filled data only. Don't worry about the cost of building an API connection; the revenue life will greatly outweigh the cost.

## Automation #9: Product Triggers

**Goal: use product status changes, such as availability, inventory levels, and price changes, to trigger personalized emails to high-intent subscribers and affinity groups.**

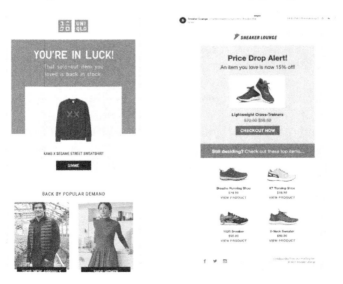

Triggered product emails are another fantastic set of automations. Since there are quite a few emails in this realm - including new arrivals, back in stock, and price drops - I grouped them into an overall automation set.

Product triggers are pretty self-explanatory, but they can be challenging to turn on without a steady, scheduled flow of product data. Here are a few of the most popular and most profitable triggers:

- **Back in Stock** - triggered when an out-of-stock item comes back in stock
- **New Arrival** - triggered when an item goes live on site
- **Low Stock** - triggered when an item's inventory level drops below a certain threshold
- **Price Drop** - triggered when an item's price drops a set amount or percentage
- **New Reviews** - triggered when a new review is added for an item

You can probably identify even more product triggers related to your business based on these top five. Since all of these triggers are primarily the same look & style, aside from the theme, I'll outline the key elements to make these consistently successful across the board:

**Consistent, Clean Product Feeds = Great Triggers.**

Ensure your product feeds are coming in consistently with the latest product data. For example, sending a Back in Stock email for a popular product when the product didn't have enough stock to cover the mailbase is going to have a lot of angry customers.

An example of a trigger gone wrong is when the Apple Airpods Pro came out; we got about 1,000 pre-orders, yet when the inventory came live, we could only fulfill 200 pre-orders to start;

unfortunately, the Back in Stock email launched to all 1,000 and more, leading to a lot of disappointed customers!

Another example would be sending a price drop email before realizing that the price changed back to the regular price with the next hourly feed.

These are isolated examples, of course, but definitely some of the hard lessons I've encountered. Usually, the best way to power product triggers is through a clean API or CSV feed to your ESP.

Some brands power full product catalog data feeds every day with hourly delta feeds (feeds with only select product changes instead of the full product catalog), while others prefer APIs every time there's a product change. Some ESPs help fill the gap by scraping the website and adapting to real-time product edits.

No matter how you approach the data needed to power your triggers, be sure they're as consistent and as real-time as possible, so the customer isn't disappointed by misinformation when they click back to site.

**Go Beyond Self-Selecting Segments.**

Let's take an email like Back in Stock for the Apple Airpods Pro. Most brands trigger this email to customers who opt-in - or self-select - to receive a back-in-stock alert. Makes sense since self-selection is one of the highest-intent buying signals you'll receive! It may be a small segment, but definitely powerful.

You can expand that audience beyond self-selection, though. Think of all the subscribers who've viewed the item, carted the item, and even searched for the item while it was out of stock. Those subscribers would be a great audience since they showed a signal of buying intent as well; as such, include them in your Back in Stock campaign.

I can go even deeper and include Apple loyalists, subscribers who browsed headphones or bought Apple Airpods more than 6 months ago, to name a few additional audiences. These "affinity" segments are highly valuable and expand your audience beyond just that self-selecting segment. Sending a back-in-stock email to those affinity audiences is a great source of incremental revenue.

Take a new arrival item like the new Apple iPad Pro. If I just sent an email to the "Alert When In Stock" self-selection audience, I'd reach just a tenth of the audience interested in the product. The affinity audiences for the Apple iPad Pro - like Apple loyalists, iPad buyers who should upgrade to Pro or Macbook buyers - will allow me to hit a larger population of interested buyers, triple my engagement and increase my sales.

Don't just fall back to self-selection for your product triggers; expand beyond and learn which incremental audiences drive the most revenue lift for your triggers.

## Automation #10: Transactional

**Goal: use transactional emails to provide an additional lift in personalization, leading to an increase in revenue.**

Let's first talk about the definition of transactional emails. I've talked this over with numerous e-commerce leaders over the years - from CTOs to CEOs to Heads of Customer Service to ESP Founders - and I basically came to one conclusion: no one really knows the definition of a transactional email.

Some say that transactional emails are "customer-triggered emails" while others group post-purchase emails under transactional, even upsells and product reviews. There never seemed to be any standardization across the board.

So, after reviewing the industry data, scoping out competitors and friendly emails, testing different solutions, and analyzing the trends, I came to a super-simple definition that I could explain to a five-year-old!

**Transactional emails are emails that a customer expects to receive.** Customer placed an order? They expect to receive an order confirmation. Lost their password? The customer expects to receive a password reset email. Shipping delays? The customer needs a shipping update email. These are all samples of transactional emails, and they fit the bill as expected forms of communication, triggered by the user or not.

Why is this important? Because transactional emails provide the highest engagement rates of any campaign, guaranteeing a highly receptive and engaged recipient. Delicately balancing the transactional and promotional elements within these emails is the next challenge. Here are some tips to maximize the opportunities of your transactional emails.

**Recommendations Work Wonders.**

Monetizing transactional emails comes down to one word: recommendations. Check out the bottom of two of the order confirmation emails I got from Best Buy and Wayfair (I masked the order specifics for privacy reasons).

Notice how the bottom of every email contains additional products "related to my purchase." Needless to say, these recommendations were very helpful and personalized, and I never once thought that these brands overstepped their transactional boundaries. Best Buy even went further; they invited me to join their email list (I'm already on it, but this is great if I wasn't) and soft-sold me on their Outlet deals.

If you've A/B tested product recommendation emails against non-product recommendations emails, you'll know that recommendations provide a great incremental lift for your program. I saw a 30% increase in revenue due to product recs.

Multiply those product recs across five or six transactional emails - messages that are sent to both subscribers and non-subscribers, and we're talking about a really great source of revenue for you… while also being super-relevant for customers.

## Transactional Goes Beyond Orders.

Ever noticed that brands have updates to their privacy policy quite often? Check out some of the emails I got over the years about updates.

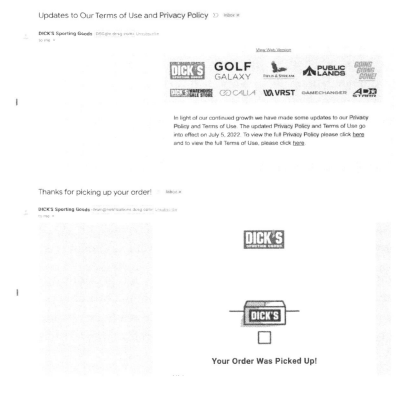

These "privacy policy updates" are a great example of a transactional email that's not related to a purchase. Check out the examples from Dick's Sporting Goods: note that the first email is from their promotional domain while the second email is from their transactional domain.

From a marketing point of view, you can use transactional emails like these to re-engage and re-activate your list. Sending a privacy policy update to your full list - which is an entirely legal and important update for subscribers - increases engagement rates from users you haven't heard from in months.

From a marketing point of view, you can use transactional emails like these to re-engage and re-activate your list. Sending a privacy policy update to your full list - which is an entirely legal and important update for subscribers - increases engagement rates from users you haven't heard from in months.

I'll give another example of a non-purchase-related email: customer survey. Although this is timed to run an hour or two after purchase, a customer survey is a two or three-step shopping experience questionnaire that yields 75% open rates and 30% click rates while also generating actual useful data from customers.

Think about all the forms of customer communication that can be categorized as transactional. Once you map those out, consider how personalized recommendations can improve the customer experience while benefiting your bottom line at the same time. This is truly the Multiplication part of the S.P.A.M. Strategy and is extremely powerful when layered into transactional automations.

*** 

By incorporating the S.P.A.M. Strategy into these top ten automations, your email, SMS and CRM program will quickly ascend to the top 10% of e-commerce brands. You'll free up a huge amount of time and effort while creating an automated source of revenue and profits. In addition, your customers will experience a hyper-relevant approach within every email and SMS touchpoint and truly appreciate the personalization efforts your brand is putting forth.

You've officially made it to the end of this book. You've unlocked the power of the S.P.A.M. Strategy, amplified it with email and SMS applications, learned how the Post-Purchase Hourglass turns one-time buyers into lifetime buyers, and automated your revenue streams 24/7/365 with the top ten automations.

You're now on the path to creating a high-performing customer-centric email and SMS program for your business. But before you do, be prepared for a couple more challenges that I'll help you overcome in the next chapter.

## Swipe & Deploy Guide: Top Ten Automations

Need a deeper look at how to create these top ten automations? Then download our free Top Ten Automations Swipe & Deploy Guide. In this workbook, I'll share visuals on how your automations should look, and tips on expanding them beyond the out-of-the-box ESP versions. In addition, you can send an email to isaac@hiflyerdigital.com with the subject line "Swipe and Deploy automations," and I'll gladly drop a few of these automations right into your Klaviyo account for free. Download the Top Ten Automations Swipe and Deploy Guide by visiting HiFlyerDigital.com/automations.

# CONCLUSION

You've officially made it to the end of this book and learned how to create a profitable, predictable, and sustainable revenue stream from email & SMS for your brand.

If I had a certificate to share with you, I would gladly send it! In fact, if you email me at isaac@hiflyerdigital.com and mention that you've completed the book, I'll gladly send you a special gift as a thank you. Would love to hear your feedback on this book as well - or a positive review online also - so be sure to shoot me that email.

Let's recap what I shared in this book. Together, we have:

1. Demystified the seven main reasons why customers will leave your business this year for your competitors.
2. Clarified why email & SMS is the best way of leveling the playing field and why retention is critical NOW.
3. Highlighted the top reasons for why brands fail at email & SMS and how to recalibrate your own preconceptions.
4. Outlined the important building blocks for a data-driven, customer-centric, and profitable email & SMS program.
5. Revealed the secret email & SMS strategy of the top 1% - which we playfully call our S.P.A.M. Strategy.

6. Embraced the marketing creed of "right person, right message, right time, repeat" and committed ourselves to honoring it.
7. Illustrated how the S.P.A.M. Strategy yielded great revenue results... as well as added benefits and measurables such as reduced unsubscribe rates, fewer emails sent, and lower ad costs.
8. Crafted the perfect blend of creative, context, and conversion optimized links to "explode" clicks and sales
9. Mapped out a Post-Purchase Hourglass approach that will turn one-time buyers into lifetime buyers
10. Shared the Top 10 Email & SMS Automations for E-commerce that will grow revenues on autopilot.
11. Positioned YOUR BRAND for immense success simply because you completed this book!

Now's the time to roll up your sleeves and start implementing these strategies immediately. Having been in your shoes, I can guarantee that you'll face the following challenges immediately:

1. **Data and Technology Challenges** - it's frustrating when you're ready to run, and you realize that the data isn't clean or the tech isn't performing as well as you'd like.
2. **Company / Team Pushback** - trying to convince your internal team, ownership, or even co-workers about all the changes you want to initiate could cause a lot of friction and pushback; no one likes change!
3. **Shiny New Object Syndrome** - you'll be distracted by new initiatives, new tech, and ways to expand on what you've learned before fully implementing the S.P.A.M. Strategy from start to finish.

I've been there. I know how it feels to get slowed down, challenged, and distracted. Stay the course, though. The customer should always be at the center of what you do. Even if your brand or company isn't ready yet, you've personally taken a major leap forward by completing this book.

As a natural visionary, I tend to be very strategic, aspirational, and very "high level." But I also know that for the sake of my clients, employees, and followers, I need to bring those high-level visionary strategies down to "eye level" and provide a tactical, organized, and planned rollout of the S.P.A.M. Strategy.

For that reason, I created a 12-month Email & SMS Roadmap to help clarify where our email and SMS program was trying to go and what steps we would take monthly to get there.

**Our 12-month Email, SMS & CRM Roadmap will help you and your team:**

- Set your foundation
- Stay on track
- Create SMART goals
- Achieve wins early
- Automate workloads
- Remove distractions
- Help get buy-in from other teams

A 12-month roadmap will help you:

1. Focus on the foundation and get all your tools, data, and tech in order so you can confidently get a running start.
2. Get buy-in from all the stakeholders when they see what steps, requests, and requirements look like, allowing them to share feedback and feel involved.
3. Reduces distractions from new vendors, tech, and internal teams because everyone can see the roadmap and, together, can commit to getting there in unison.

I'm more than happy to share my 12-month Email & SMS Roadmap with you to help you stay organized. Simply go to hiflyerdigital.com/roadmap for a free copy

Of course, considering HiFlyer Digital runs the email, SMS and CRM strategy for 7, 8, 9, and 10-figure brands, I'm more than happy to jump on a call directly with you and your team to outline exactly what you're doing well, where there is room for improvement and how we partner with you to hit the next level.

As a small yet scaling business myself, I believe you have the power to change the world, and it starts with changing the relationship with your customers. If I can help you build better customer relationships, your customers will be happier, your employees will feel empowered, and your business will be more successful than ever before. That's the power of you, the small business. Good luck and remember…

**It's not about the email. It's about the person behind the email. Build a relationship with THAT person.**

Printed in Great Britain
by Amazon

25095376R00188